Go Phish

Dave Thompson

St. Martin's Griffin
New York

Book design by Scott Levine

Library of Congress Cataloging-in-Publication Data

Thompson, Dave.
    Go Phish / Dave Thompson.
        p.   cm.
    ISBN 0-312-16854-3
    1. Phish (Musical group)   2. Rock musicians—United
States—Biography.   I. Title.
ML421.P565T5   1997
782.42166'092'2—dc21
    [B]   97-2743
                                                 CIP
                                                 MN

10   9   8   7   6   5

Contents

ACKNOWLEDGMENTS

"Burlington," Page McConnell once mused of Phish's hometown, "lends itself to having a great music scene. Because it's an isolated town way up there, there are no other places to go for entertainment. Cycles of bands pop up, become popular, and then fall off for a while, and then other groups of bands get together and there'll be another scene."

Trey Anastasio agreed. "Vermont has everything to do with who we are. Simplicity and slowness. And cold. People here are in no rush to get anywhere."

That is certainly true of Phish, just as it is true of their fans, the devoted army that media convention has irredeemably christened Phish Heads, and whose very existence ensures that no retelling of this incredible band's story could be complete without them. This book is no exception; it is through the vast repository of oral law which surrounds Phish that the unwritten history of thirteen years of performing can be told.

It is, in the words of the old cliché, a journey into the heart of rock 'n' roll, and an exploration of the mechanics of a modern rock phenomenon. Because it is Phish, however, it is also an explanation of how those mechanics can be by-passed.

They have never, for instance, fit into any kind of scene; even their much publicized alliance with the H.O.R.D.E. traveling circus owes more to other people's perceptions of the group than to any concrete affirmation, and this is as true today, when Phish are exploding across international stages, as it was in the mid-1980s, when their appeal remained purely local. Even when a Vermont "scene" did look to be emerging, Phish remained gleefully out of the loop. "There was this upheaval of Burlington bands, where suddenly Burlington was going to be the next Athens, Georgia," recalls Trey. "We were just ignored by everyone. They had this big festival which featured all the local bands, and we weren't invited. . . ."

There are other examples of Phish's independence. As the music industry tightens its grip on every aspect of merchandising, with bootleg manufacturers being busted almost weekly, Phish encourage their fans to tape every concert they play.

It doesn't appear to have hurt them any. The group's "official" albums have between them sold over a million copies, but there are more than five hundred live cassettes in circulation, traveling the vast Phish underground network. Maybe the band are, as one of their record company executives recently insisted, "cutting their own throat"; but as Phish themselves replied, "At least it's us holding the razor."

"As one tries to establish oneself in this industry, it's easy to get influenced," keyboard player Page McConnell says. "Different people want to get you to do different things. It's a business to most people [and] in the push and pull, you're bound to bend a little bit. But we've started to take everything back. It's our career. We're only going to do what makes us happy."

It is this uncompromising stance, a refusal to toe the record-company line and rehearse their ad-libs to the point of routine staleness, which sets Phish so far apart from their peers—which has always been the band's strongest card.

Phish know their audience, and they understand them. Phish Heads are not the kind of people who attend one gig every tour, and then go home to play the album over cocktails. They are devoted and demanding, and they are not alone in their mania. At every show, countless armies of Phish Heads have traveled cross-country to be there, and the group repay this loyalty by ensuring that ticket prices never even hint at the exorbitant sums commanded by other touring bands—prices seldom exceed $25 in fact; a truly magnanimous gesture given the size of Phish's onstage set up and offstage entourage.

"Too many fans follow us to every show." Page McConnell reiterates the loyalty which has done so much to establish Phish. "They couldn't afford it if we charged 'real' ticket prices."

This altruism permeates every aspect of Phish's public persona. "They're a performing group," McConnell's research scientist father says. "They don't read critiques, don't care about gold and platinum records. They want to have fun."

The Phish Heads, of course, are only one of the sources for this biography. Without the eyes and ears of an enormous cast of phriends, phans, and phellow travelers, the decade's worth of work and play which has brought Phish to their present plateau of success could never have been completed. I would like to take this opportunity, then, to thank everybody who shared their time and memories with me, in person, by telephone, or over the Internet—you know who you are.

Shell, Carl, and Tiffany (is it an *i* or a *y*?), in particular, deserve an especial vote of gratitude; so, for gifting the world with such a magnificent work of reference, does the staff of, and contributors to, *The Pharmer's Almanac: The UnoPHicial Guide to the Band* (Pharmer's Almanac, 1996). Dean Budnick's similarly structured *The Phishing Manual—A Compendium to the Music of Phish* (Hyperion, 1996) was also a valuable resource.

Several magazines kept the Phish phaith strong, and were of immense assistance during my researches: *Relix, Dupree's Diamond News*, and *Unbroken Chain* lead the pack, but I should also acknowledge *Rolling Stone, Gallery of Sound Gazette, Bass Player* magazine, *Goldmine, Live! Music Review, The New Yorker, Entertainment Weekly*, and the *Boston Globe*. And then, of course, there's Phish's own *Doniac Schvice* newsletter, and the Phish Net. Beth and Rick at the Landing in Seattle get a massive round of applause; and, for other favors great and small, further thanks to Anchorite Man; Bateerz, Scary, and Baby Bats; Shawn Brice, Tony DiMaggio; Karen Domerski; Drum Tobacco; Barb East; Ella; Bill Glahn and all at *Live! Music Review*; the Gremlins who live in the furnace; K-Mart (not the store); Kiss the Stone for keeping music live; ace designer Scott Levine; Alex Mulcahey and *Gallery of Sound Gazette*; Geoff Monmouth; Tony Nolan; Oedipus; Orifice; Saul Penman and his amazing bathing costume (huh?); Jane Regina; Doug Rotondo; Snarleyyow; Spiny Norman; Sprocket; and the ultra-mysterious Dame Gaiety Tomcat.

My editor, Greg Cohn, and agent, Madeleine Morel; Gaye and Tim; Jo-Ann Greene; Brian Gross; Chris Nickson; Brian Perera; all of whom, without whom . . . And finally, Amy, who now knows more about Phish than she ever thought she needed to.

GONE GHOTI-ING

Nobody seemed to be quite sure what was happening. Around the corners of the room, a few uniformed buzzcuts sank beers and postured, while the girls they'd attracted fluttered impatiently toward the dance floor.

In the half-darkness of his hideaway, the disc jockey played some loud Michael Jackson, and "Wanna Be Startin' Something" came bouncing off the walls. Onstage, the four guys who'd been chopping through a distinctly restless Marvin Gaye cover blinked uncertainly at one another and wondered where they'd gone wrong.

Near the front, a girl whooped support; everyone looked, but they'd seen her already, the only person in the whole damned room who'd even tried to dance to the rickety music, and as the musicians put down their instruments and wandered off the stage, a dull thump administered the coup de grace to their concert. It was the sound of a hockey stick disentangling itself from the mass of duct tape which once held it in place, and falling off the stage.

"It's hard to ignore a hint like that!" The drummer, squinting through the veil of sweat which hung behind his spectacles, gestured one thumb in the direction of the music. "But at least it was Michael Jackson blowing us offstage."

Amy Skelton, the girl from the front of the stage, finally wandered up to join them. "I thought you were great," she smiled, and if she was lying, it didn't really show. "It was your first gig, after all."

The guitarist smiled back. "Which means you're our first fan. Welcome to the club."

The quartet drank up, then left the room. There was another show booked in just a few days, and unless they wanted a repeat of tonight, they had some serious thinking, and playing, to do. As they parted for the evening, there was just one last thing to say to each other. "Happy Halloween." Overhead, the cloudy Vermont sky was wondering whether to snow.

A sudden rush of classical architecture in the state the developers forgot, the University of Vermont in Burlington sprawls across the landscape like a Degas ballerina. From the wooded campus, Lake Champlain offers a respite from the forests and hills which roll through the state, and though the university— the fifth-oldest in the country—ranks among the most respected in America, the academic requirements it makes of its 10,000 students are nothing compared to the climatic demands.

Vermont itself was named by the French explorer after whom the lake is named, Samuel de Champlain: Ver-, from the French word for "green," *verd*; -mont for "mountain," *mont*. But he was there in the summer, when all is a wonderland of rolling verdant forest; he stayed through the fall, and the kaleidoscopic leaf show which decorates the woodland with nature's own psychedelic light show. By October, the snows have already started falling; by Christmas, the place is a sea of white. Come Easter, and one doesn't even think about Vermont without packing a ski suit first.

There is a calmness there, though, which defies even the boisterous blur of the winter sportsmen, and a hardiness which the urban sprawls farther south ofttimes mistake for simplicity. *Vermont*, reads a typical introduction, *the home of Ethan Allen and Ben and Jerry's ice cream*, and a bumper sticker paraphrases insistently, *"You don't have to be laid-back to live here, but it helps."*

Climbing, skiing, trapping, hunting—entire communities exist around those pastimes, drawing the tourists in through the summer, then rolling up the sidewalks and sleeping through the cold. Others, even more self-contained and self-sustaining, don't even need the tourists, and those they do meet have either become lost, or are hoping to. Through the late 1960s, the wooded border with Quebec was a favorite haunt of America's draft-dodgers, pouring up Highway 91 as it paced the famous Rock Island Line, or skewing off onto roads which were little more than rutted tracks, passing unseen into Canada, and a world without war.

A lot of them made it, but a lot didn't need to, as they vanished into the countryside to wait out the slaughter, blending into the soil, and the lifestyle came quickly. They're still up there now, walking museums of Vietnam Vintage, the old VW bus grittily doing her duty, and once in a while, they'll track into town, to buy what they need and barter for more. *"You don't have to be self-sufficient to live here, but it helps."* And while Dropping Out of Society isn't on the UVM curriculum, there are not many students there who wouldn't know how it's done.

Just another long-haired freshman with a bass guitar in his luggage, Mike Gordon arrived in Vermont in September, 1983. He was eighteen, fresh out of Sudbury, Massachusetts, but Burlington made him feel ancient. Maybe it was the nonstop diet of grizzled classic-rockers which began pumping out of the radio the moment he crossed the state line that did it, or maybe it was the knowledge that from now until he graduated, the best thing he could hope for was that MTV would follow him out there. But whatever it was, he didn't like it.

Born in Boston on June 3, 1965, Mike Gordon's hobby was organizing things. He'd been doing it since he was tiny, and in later years he would look back and reason, "I probably didn't feel like I had enough control, so I decided to make up these fantasy things that I could control."

Control was the operative word. One day, Mike recruited a couple of friends to help him build a go-cart, and it was the most natural thing in the world that the cart became a sports car, and that one car became an entire fleet of the things, lined up in the forecourt of his young imagination, streamlined, gleaming, and costing an absolute fortune. Soon, he knew, the whole world would be dreaming of owning a Hawk, a streamlined, gleaming, magenta Hawk.

"Magenta?" There was dissension in the ranks already. "Magenta?" Two against one. But it was Mike's car, Mike's dream, and that question mark at the end of the word, that was fighting talk. "Yeah, magenta. Do you have a problem with that?"

Later, he could laugh, but at the time it was serious. "I wanted magenta, they didn't. So I threatened to quit. Of course they couldn't do without me, so they said magenta would have to do." And with that decided, they went home for dinner, and the Hawk was never mentioned again.

"My interests would change every two weeks," Mike recalls. "I liked to spend a lot of time alone, always working on projects, but after two weeks, I would realize that my interest was changing, I had a new project I wanted to work on, and I wouldn't know what the new one was; it was always frustrating to figure out, 'What do I want to be doing now?'"

He would always figure it out in the end, of course, but

until he did, he was antsy, impatient, his face furrowed thoughtfully and his brain racing around like a mad thing. At times like that, nothing could get through to him, not his parents, not his brother, and most of all, not school.

Solomon Schecter Day School, in Mike's hometown of Sudbury, Massachusetts, was strict, and strictly Jewish. From third grade on, everybody spoke Hebrew for half a day, every day, with ingenious punishments being meted out to anyone who didn't—or couldn't—comply. Mike was one of the ones who couldn't. When everyone else in his class was fluent, he was struggling to grasp hold of the basics.

He excuses himself with a laugh. "Imagine a kid who doesn't know Hebrew, listening to a twenty-minute Hebrew lecture!"

He diverted himself by dreaming and scheming. "I didn't want to be a kid, I wanted to be an adult." He still possesses the filing cabinet stuffed with documents that were his childhood delight, drawers full of "typed plans for clubs, different kinds of clubs."

There were hundreds of them, including a few he actually put into practice, and one, just one, which he'd even call successful. "That was this one called the Social Club. There were six of us in the neighborhood, and every Monday after school we had a meeting. We taped it. I still have the tapes. We had an agenda to talk about, and we had donations. We had one field trip." And then it fizzled out. Another time, Mike decided he wanted to make movies. He formed a moviemakers' club. One script was written, and then he moved on. He fell in love with electronics, and there was an electronics club.

At first, music was just another of these passing fancies. By his own admission, Mike was never particularly promiscuous in his musical tastes: He'd played piano since he was six, but "growing up, the first album I ever listened to was

5

[the Beatles'] *Abbey Road*. My first few years, that was the only album that I ever listened to."

Songs like George Harrison's plaintive "Something," Ringo Starr's whimsical "Octopus's Garden," and John Lennon's megalithic "I Want You (She's So Heavy)," the last notes the Beatles ever recorded for release, remain branded on his consciousness to this day. But at the time, that's all they were, songs. Not until his early teens did he also begin to see them as a means of escape, from the closeted world he was erecting around himself, and from the rigors of the real world beyond. He had transferred to public school, and it was hell.

"In Solomon Schecter, no discipline was ever needed because nobody ever did anything wrong, and everyone was brilliant. Then, suddenly, I was in a school where the main thing was to beat each other up, do drugs, and peel out in the parking lot. I was the one in charge of getting beaten up; one day I was walking down the hall, and this tall ratty kid said to me, 'I hate your face,' and he punched me."

With music, for the first time, he was able to "branch out a little bit." He talked about forming a band in the same spirit he'd once talked about an electronics club, but when this dream came to fruition, he stuck with it. Music became his life, and his life began to focus around music.

Mike gravitated toward the bass guitar because "you can vibrate people" with it. On holiday in the Bahamas with his parents and brother in 1979, the fourteen-year-old stood by the hotel swimming pool with his father while the house group, the Mustangs, ran through their repertoire of Top-40 favorites. "And the bass could just vibrate you," Mike recalls. "The guitar could make pretty melodies, but the bass could actually vibrate your whole body. I really liked that physical thing, and I told my dad at that point that if I were ever in a band when I got older, that I would want to play bass."

By his early teens, that dream was coming true. In his

bedroom at night, Mike would lock the door and then climb into the big black box he'd suspended from the ceiling, and sit there practicing his rented Beatle bass copy. Alone in this self-contained environment, free from even the most insignificant visual distraction, he played . . . he vibrated. And when he emerged, to form his first group, Mike's father, the man who founded Massachusetts's Store 24 chain, didn't even bat an eyelid. Instead, he loaned his son the use of a company van to drive the band's gear around in.

For the first time in his life, Mike reflects, "I was more in a social situation. All my friends in high school were people in the band or friends of my high-school band."

That was the Tombstone Blues Band, an adventurous combo that specialized in blues and sixties rock, partly because of Mike's growing admiration for Peter Albin, bass player with Janis Joplin's San Francisco aggregation, Big Brother and the Holding Company; but more out of deference to one of Tombstone's other members, Cary.

Cary's father once played with bluesman Muddy Waters, and Mike openly admits, "His dad was better than him"—so much better that there was actually a plot for father to replace son in the lineup! And when it failed, the Tombstone Blues Band had dug its own grave.

Still at high school, Mike's next outfit was the Edge. It was the late 1970s by now, and rock's post-punk New Wave, ricocheting out of nearby Boston, slammed straight into the young bassist's consciousness. "We had some originals," Mike recollects, but the band's repertoire was more comfortable with contemporary covers: Talking Heads, the Police, the Pretenders, and so forth. The Edge went west when Mike moved north, and he arrived at UVM with only one goal, finding himself a new group.

Looking back, he explains, "I'd been doing music, and instead of having a hundred different interests like most Geminis have, I guess I just started concentrating on music." It was hard enough, he sighed, simply to balance his two musical goals, "bass playing and songwriting," without having to worry about everything else that interested him, "filmmaking and all the other things."

His only distraction was the course he was signed up to study, electrical engineering, and even there appeared an inexplicable, perfect dovetailing. "The head of the electrical-engineering department said that there were a lot of engineers that were bass players, according to what he had found." The professor offered no explanation for this phenomenon. It was, simply, a fact of life.

Even in his first few weeks at college, Mike quickly came to realize there were always a few bands knocking around the campus, unambitious aggregations for the most part, looking to play a few songs, pick up a few girls, whatever it took to quell raging teenage hormones. That was pretty much all he wanted to do, too, when he followed through on a flyer he'd seen flapping in one of the halls.

Like Mike, Ernest Giuseppe Anastasio III, "Trey," was a freshman, grimly coming to terms with Burlington, Vermont. His first impressions did not give the state much hope of impressing him; Vermont, he decided, "was just longhairs who lived out in the country and hiked a lot." He didn't know what they did for fun in these parts, but the glazed expressions he caught around campus and the furtive goings-on he saw in certain corners didn't leave too much room for the imagination. Particularly as his newfound best friend, an affable hobbit whose friends called him Fish, had already made it clear what his hobby was. God bless Timothy Leary.

Fresh-faced and bespectacled, short-haired and city-smart, there was still a barely perceptible trace of Texas in

Trey's accent. He'd left his Fort Worth birthplace when he was two, though, and since then, he'd divided his life between the family home in Princeton, New Jersey, and a private prep school in Watertown, Connecticut.

His family background was impressive. His father, Ernest Anastasio II, was executive vice president of Educational Testing Services, the fiends who set the SAT exams. His mother, Diane, was an editor on *Sesame Street* magazine. With or without the all-consuming passion for music which no one around him could fail to register, Trey (a nickname derived from the numeral that follows his given name) was clearly destined to go far.

Trey commenced his musical career playing drums, eight years old and hammering hell out of anything that stayed in one place long enough for him to get some kind of rhythm going. He was a child when his first song was recorded, as well, when his mother announced she was involved in compiling an album for the children's educational market. Catching Trey as he wandered around the house singing the self-composed nonsense he delighted in creating, she sat him down for his first lesson in songwriting. The result, the tale of an impetuous frog named Joe, would appear on a collection of ditties called *Sing and Learn Large Motor Skills*.

Once bitten, never shy, a decade later, Trey continued writing songs, only now he was banging them out with his Princeton Day School buddies, and stockpiling them for the day they might come in useful. Many of Trey's earliest songs, including several he would still be playing through the first years of Phish, bear cowriting credits for his friends Bob Szuter, Aaron Woolfe, Dave Abrahams, and Marc Daubert; and then, of course, there was Tom Marshall, who continues to write songs with Trey today. When Trey earned his first gold record, for Phish's *A Live One* in-concert recording, he made certain that Princeton Day School was presented with a plaque formally acknowledging the music department's contribution to his career.

By the time he graduated from Princeton Day School, Trey had long since traded in his drumsticks, realizing very early on that although you can do a lot of things with a drum kit, songwriting is not one which springs immediately to mind. Neither is picking up girls, and what else do you go to school for? He traded in his drum kit for a guitar, and while he struggled to master the instrument, in his sophomore year at Taft Academy he joined his first band.

Red Tide was a sprawling aggregation, eight members, and eight violently clashing temperaments strong. Uncertain about his guitar playing, Trey was initially handling vocals alone, but with the remaining septet crashing aggressively away, Red Tide worked up a songbook of hard-rock covers: Deep Purple's turbulent "Smoke on the Water," Cream's monolithic "Sunshine of Your Love" . . . if a song packed enough testosterone, Red Tide would tackle it and pound it into the ground.

The musical differences which were to sunder Red Tide sprang fully-formed from their repertoire. Half the members' tastes sprang from Headbanger Central, half from the more adventurous, and maybe less aggressive musings of the Allmans and the Dead, with the divergent streams only coming together in a mutual love for Led Zeppelin. It was this half which would, three years later, unite as Space Antelope.

With Trey having finally committed himself to playing guitar, and another student, Steve Pollack, handling vocals, Space Antelope devoted itself to learning Trey and Tom Marshall's ever-burgeoning stockpile of songs, and Pollack's own efforts, a repertoire which even Trey has since described as wide but not overly impressive. It was, however, ambitious, particularly after they worked up a version of Pink Floyd's seventeen-minute opus "Dogs," and at least one new song emerged from the chaos—even if it would be another few years before it was finally written.

Steve Pollack's forte was coining bizarre couplets and phrases, slices of deep and meaningless philosophy which could reduce his bandmates to tears of laughter. "Set the gearshift for the high gear of your soul," he spouted one evening, "you've got to run like an antelope, out of control." With additional lyrics from Trey and Tom Marshall, Trey's next group, Phish, would include "Run Like an Antelope" on their first-ever demo tape; more than a decade later, the song was still a regular in their live set.

"Run Like an Antelope," of course, was an exception; the remainder of Space Antelope's repertoire enjoyed nowhere near as much longevity. But it was a start, and one which not only confirmed Trey's ambition, to be making music, it also cemented two valuable, lasting friendships. Today, more than two decades after they met, Tom Marshall and Trey still write songs together, while Steve Pollack would become the ubiquitous Dude of Life, longtime Phish coconspirator, and, for many fans, the physical embodiment of the band's musical doctrine. Anarchic, comical, sometimes even embarrassing, the Dude of Life represents the free-spirited totem around which the Phish community would eventually develop.

All of that, of course, was far off in an unknown future when school broke up in the summer of 1983 and took Space Antelope with it. Almost before he'd even finished unpacking, on his first day at UVM, Trey's only thought was to find a new lineup to work with.

He did not have far to look. A year older than Trey, Jeff Holdsworth was a sophomore electrical-engineering student, a guitarist who avidly shared Trey's taste in music: the Dead, the Allmans, Led Zeppelin. They began playing together, marveling at the ease with which their individual styles dovetailed. Together, they began scouring the campus for any like-minded musicians.

UVM's Redstone campus, like campuses all over America, was awash with players. Every classroom, every corridor, every corner, nurtured another musician, another ambition; and through the walls of his dormitory, late into the night, Trey could hear them playing, plotting, and on one occasion drumming, very loudly, very persuasively. Intrigued, he followed the sound to its source. There he found Fish.

A process of elimination pruned Jonathan Fishman's name down to what it became. To his parents and elders, it was his first name which contracted; to his contemporaries, it was his last. Somehow, "Fish" seemed to suit the slightly short, slightly dumpy, slightly shortsighted young man a lot better.

In years to come, a visiting journalist would describe the mild-mannered Fish as resembling "something out of *Lord of the Rings*," and Fish, cuddly, bearded, bespectacled, smiled because he'd heard it all before. The first time Trey set eyes on Fish, having followed the clatter through the dormitory walls, the guitarist just pointed at his discovery and fell over laughing. Fish was, Trey insisted afterward, "the funniest-looking guy I'd ever seen."

Hailing from Philadelphia, where he was born on February 26, 1965, Fish was six months younger than Trey. His adoptive parents were both artists—his orthodontist father sculpted; his mother, Mimi, painted—and just like the Anastasio clan, when their eight-year-old son began expressing an interest in playing drums, they simply stocked up on headache remedies and let him get on with it.

Fish would be thirteen before he started taking formal drum lessons, by which time he was already hammering his way through at least one set of Led Zeppelin albums. When he reached college, he was happily rehearsing eight hours a day, seeking out every challenge he could find and persisting until he could match it.

His musical influences, he happily admitted, sprawled all over the place, from the stark, snare-led minimalism of the Velvet Underground's Maureen Tucker, through to the absurd syncopations of Bill Bruford, the percussive dynamo behind early Yes and the most intriguing King Crimson, then on into the alien pastures of jazzman Sun Ra. One night, Fish set himself to learning Genesis's "Apocalypse in 9/8," the most thunderous movement from that band's "Supper's Ready" suite; another, he would be grappling with King Crimson's "Talking Drum." What was remarkable was that he never gave up till he'd figured it out. What was even more remarkable was that he always did figure it out.

Like Trey's guitar, Fish's drums were an all-consuming passion. In sports, he excelled at swimming, learning for himself the muscular benefits which could be applied to his instrument. And at play, he quickly discovered that if you really needed to get high, LSD beat grass any day. Smoking, he averred, "was a cardiovascular issue . . . so I was into tripping."

It worked for him as well. The ensuing combination of acid and percussion made for some mind-boggling excursions, and he would happily acknowledge, "My first experiences inspired me to play—it was like graduating." It was only later, after meeting Trey, that he began to notice the downside to his decision.

"When you're high, your playing seems to sound better, but when you listen back to the tapes, it sucks. I ended up stopping quickly because I would have one experience or another where drugs would end my ability to play. The drug becomes a pain in the ass when you have to do your homework and learn something new. It blocks you up and makes it harder to learn something." And Trey, keen to the point of evangelistic fervor, always wanted him to learn something new. The pair established their common musical ground within the first few hours of meeting. Now it was time to seek out new frontiers of expression.

Within days, the flyers which caught Mike Gordon's eye were springing up around the campus, calling for adventurous musicians with an ear for . . . the Grateful Dead were apparently mentioned (in conversation, if not on the posters), Frank Zappa, the Allman Brothers, and a rogues' gallery of combos whose musical heyday came and went before most UVM students even hit high school. But that wasn't the point. The early 1980s enjoyed their musical moments, of course, but compared to the sounds which passed by before, it was all so much window-dressing. If you wanted to put things bluntly, it came down to a straight choice: Duran Duran or "Dark Star," and Trey, Jeff, and Fish knew precisely where they wanted to fly.

By the end of the week, Mike was wandering into the never-ending public jam session which was the trio's idea of an audition, and was quickly invited to stay. It was taking place in a dormitory lounge, with something like twenty-five other people standing around and dancing. Baffled, but intrigued, Mike played to the end of the session, then walked over to the others. "So, do I get the job?"

"I got the job," he laughs.

"It's funny," he reflects years later, "because the first time we jammed together, it didn't really click. There were other people I had jammed with where I felt it had clicked better." But he decided to persevere anyway, and with the lineup now complete, all they needed was a name.

That came easily enough. Fish was already the best-known face on campus; they simply named the group after him.

That's one theory, anyway. Another is that they were paying obscure tribute to a Dead alumnus, bassist Phi[l Le]sh—Mike has never disguised his admiration for Lesh's playing. Another still insists they worked around one of author George Bernard Shaw's theories on the absurdity of the English language, an observation based around the fact that the word *fish* could, and maybe should, be spelled *ghoti*.

Phonetically, at least, Shaw's theory is sound: the *f* sound can be found in *trough*; the *i* in *women*; the *sh* in *Martian*. Historically, however, that tale could be called a crock of *tioed*. According to Fish, "When it was time to decide a name for the band, I suggested the sound of an airplane taking off—'phssssh.' But then we thought that we needed a vowel. Imagine people saying 'We're going to see Phssssh tonight.' " Yet he insists that Trey had already designed what would become Phish's famous piscine logo, and that it was purely coincidental that the *i* fit perfectly in the middle.

It was Jeff Holdsworth who landed the newly named Phish their first-ever concert. He'd seen signs around campus for an ROTC dance on October 30, 1983, and went in search of the organizers, to find out whether they needed live entertainment. Without anyone even considering the ramifications of thrusting an untested experiment into such an arena, Phish, well-rehearsed but woefully unprepared, found themselves on the bill. Nervously, they rechristened themselves Blackwood Convention for the occasion.

Even if everything went according to plan, it would have been a rudimentary performance. Phish had been playing together for a mere matter of weeks, and though their instrumental repertoire was varied and broad, even they knew that a dance band needed to play dance songs.

But in an age when Michael Jackson, Prince, and the Police ruled the roost, the repertoire Phish conjured up—AM radio standards like "I Heard It Through the Grapevine,"

"Long Cool Woman in a Black Dress," and two renditions of "Proud Mary"—was hardly inspiring, but it would have to do. So would the makeshift mike stands the musicians were still putting together when the hall's doors opened, hurriedly duct-taping hockey sticks to a table while a handful of on-lookers shot them puzzled looks.

According to popular legend, Blackwood Convention's first, and only, concert was witnessed by precisely one person, one of Fish's friends, a fellow student named Amy Skelton. ("The second week," Trey grins, "there were two people.") In fact, there were more people present, it's just that Amy was the only one who seemed to enjoy herself. Today, Amy works as the band's merchandising manager, but remains proudest when she's described as Phish's official First Fan.

Had the group been more sensitive, she might also have been their last fan. Blackwood Convention were just a handful of numbers into their set when the DJ, considerably more aware of the room's restlessness than they were, finally de-cided enough was enough. He'd been asked to run a dance, and that was what he intended doing. Waiting only for Black-wood Convention to end the song they were playing, he turned off the PA and started playing Michael Jackson's *Thriller* album instead. The dance floor promptly filled, and the four musicians made their way offstage. That made it two hints in a row, which were very hard to ignore.

SHAKY GROUND WHEN I TALK

The ROTC show was an unmitigated disaster, nobody was denying that. But it was a learning experience, too, a reminder that music is only as sincere as the beliefs that go into it. Even after all the discussion which was channeled into their initial vision, Phish had not approached their debut show with the honesty their own hearts demanded, and they paid the price of deception. As they began preparing for their next gig, just days later in the basement of the university's Slade Hall dormitory building, they swore things would be different.

This show was more to their liking, anyway. Unlike the ROTC dance, Slade Hall would fill with people who wanted more from their music than a simple soundtrack for drinking, dancing, and, hopefully, screwing; people who would understand where Phish's music was coming from. The ill-advised covers disappeared from the set; instead, the group would simply get up there and play, until they ran out of ideas, or the audience ran out of patience. When, by the end of the evening, neither had occurred, Phish were ready for their next step.

Slade Hall would become a regular stage for Phish. According to Chris Kuroda, one of the students who caught them playing whenever he could, those shows "were pretty much the only gigs that were going on," particularly as fall turned into winter, and Burlington slid into its habitual hibernation. By the new year, Phish's show was honed to the point where they were ready once more to face a far wider audience. They applied to work the Thursday-night Happy Hour at Dillon's, an off-campus frat bar in Burlington.

"When we were starting out, it was easy to get a local gig," Fish reflected. There were somewhere in the region of fifty-two different bars in Burlington, all vying for their share of the city's ten thousand–strong campus customers, and most of them willing to pay for the night's entertainment. There was no cover charge for the audience, but if the bar did good business, the entertainers would do well. "They'd give you like three hundred bucks," Fish marvels. "So you can save your money and buy equipment and stuff." So it was at Dillon's. Phish were booked to play between five and six in the evening, not the most opportune hour to attract any kind of following, but at least it was a start. The problem was, it was followed, very quickly, by what could have been an ending.

You made your own entertainment in Burlington, using whatever tools came to hand. Some people turned to drink and drugs. Others took off for a Green Mountain hike, and disappeared for days on end, following the bear tracks and beer cans into the dark depths of nature.

And others still would launch an increasingly surreal correspondence with a friend in Colorado, which ultimately led to them getting suspended from school. Trey was still to complete his first semester when he achieved that particular honor.

The story has since become an integral part of the Phish legend, swathed in as much fiction as fact. Most sources, how-

ever, agree that Trey and a friend were embroiled in an extremely bizarre game of postal one-upmanship, employing the
U.S. Mail to transport peculiar gifts to one another. It was, of
course, harmless freshman fun and games, and it would probably have remained so, were Trey not to be blessed with a
brilliant idea. At least, it felt like a brilliant idea at the time.
The fact that it was also a dreadful pun, a visual play on words
to match any he was setting to music, only increased its via-
bility.

Sneaking into the UVM anatomy lab after hours one evening, Trey made off with a severed human hand. A visit to a
local butchery procured an equally grisly sheep's heart. He
wrapped the cold fingers around the moist organ, and scrib-
bled an accompanying note: *I've got to hand it to you, you've
really got heart*. Then he bundled the whole thing up and
dropped it off at the post office, mindless, perhaps, of the
state the offering would be in by the time it completed its
arduous journey; mindless, too, of the effect such a sight
might have on the hapless postal worker who, in ways one
can only imagine, was alerted to the bizarre contents of this
package.

There are many things one is prohibited from dispatch-
ing through the U.S. Mail. Explosives, drugs, weapons, and,
for the sake of hygiene if nothing else, lumps of unpreser-
ved meat. From the post office's point of view, there was
never any doubt where the trail led back to; the perpetrator
conveniently wrote his name and return address on the
package. The UVM authorities were contacted, and Trey,
caught bloodred-handed, was suspended from school for an
entire semester.

He returned to Princeton and to the wrath of his horrified
parents, and Phish took a backseat as well. Mike and Fish did
not stop working, however; there was no way one of the

tightest rhythm sections in town was going to simply sit on its hands, and within days of Trey's departure, they formed a brand-new group of their own.

Despite the distinctly New Wave–y overtones of their name, the Dangerous Grapes did much to further Phish's own fascination with classic rock and blues standards, the Allman Brothers and Grateful Dead included. Indeed, their refusal to deviate from a strict diet of covers ensured that by the time Trey did return to Vermont, presumably chastened, but probably not too repentant, the Grapes had not only developed a following of their own, they'd developed one which far outstripped the smattering of fans Phish used to catch. Trey's suggestion that his old bandmates abandon that enterprise and return to Phish was one that would require an awful lot of thought.

Fish was the first to return. Long since converted to Trey's musical philosophies, he was actually experimenting with giving every song a distinct new beat, never repeating himself whatever he played. Any doubts he might have entertained about deserting the cozy confines of the Grapes' digestible repertoire, and striking out for the unknown, were immediately countered by the knowledge that it was the lure of the unknown which attracted him to Trey in the first place. Fish quit the Dangerous Grapes forthwith.

Mike, however, was harder to persuade.

Burlington's greatest musical advantage, the lack of any kind of competitive scene, was also its greatest disadvantage. As Fish recalls, "There was nothing to keep up with, so there was no point where any of us was really concerned with being part of a scene." And if there's no scene to begin with, there is not really any chance of escaping into a larger one. Dangerous Grapes offered Mike the chance to do what he wanted to, within confines which would only ever become as demanding as he allowed them to. A reunion with Trey and

Phish, on the other hand, not only pitted his own musical ideas against one of the strongest wills he'd ever met, it also meant that he might spend his entire college life fighting that battle.

The four musicians' musical tastes dovetailed in a remarkably similar fashion. In an age when no pop star was complete without smart suits, latex, and a cucumber codpiece, Phish were distinctly down, dirty, and denimed. At a time when you couldn't get arrested if you didn't like Van Halen, Phish acknowledged a strange penchant for jamming, following an improvisational avenue which barely flirted with the music gaining mainstream attention elsewhere. And in an era when the short, snappy syncopations of the New Romantic movement still counted for something, the Grateful Dead's influence on Phish was as profound as it would eventually become perplexing.

Very early on, at the quartet's first rehearsals, they were acknowledging the Dead's importance, not only to their own tastes, but also those of their college contemporaries. As the stack of borrowed Dead albums piled up inside their dorm rooms, *Wake of the Flood* and *Shakedown Street, From the Mars Hotel* and *Skullfuck and Roses*, so "Eyes of the World," "Fire On the Mountain," "Scarlet Begonias," "The Other One," and "Here Comes Sunshine" all slipped effortlessly into the infant Phish's vocabulary. "I was really into the Grateful Dead, and I still am," Mike acknowledges. "I don't listen to them too much, but for me they are a big influence."

Yet it was at this same early stage that the group formulated what would become the primal difference between the Dead and the young and flapping Phish. The Dead evolved from the blues, then created their own psychedelic fusion by adding other contemporary moods to the brew. Phish developed two generations later, and they, too, would seek to create a fresh fusion from disconnected reference points.

For the Dead, however, the process was organic, almost accidental. They stumbled upon what they created, pioneers in the truest musical sense. Phish would not have that same luxury; knowing that so much had already been done in the past, aware that the quest for true originality could no longer be embarked upon with a headful of acid and no other cares in the world, Phish were forced to search out their hybrids, then drag them screaming into focus.

In purely musical terms, that boiled down to one primary difference, and one which has forever separated Phish from the band with whom they are most commonly compared. Phish have more influences than the Dead could ever have counted, but the Dead knew more about the ones they had. The Dead made music, which in turn became art. For Phish, art would always be ahead of the game. Or at least, it would try to be. Mike, however, nurtured other ideas.

Almost from the moment he was accepted into the lineup, Mike was gleefully mixing things up, disrupting any dreams and schemes that his newfound bandmates might already have concocted, and throwing ideas of his own into the nascent soup.

Their very first rehearsals together left feathers feeling ruffled, as Trey and Mike in particular first experienced the friction that would ultimately become one of their greatest musical strengths, but which was then a brand-new sensation. Both men were leaders; both, in their own way, were accustomed to having their own voices heard. The conflicts which emerged at those earliest sessions remain a vital part of their relationship today. So do the solutions they arrived at.

Trey listened to jazz, the classics, a lot of improvisational music. Asked to reel off his influences, names like Sun Ra and Miles Davis lay side by side with the Velvet Underground. Mike, on the other hand, preferred rock, pure and simple, shot through with the funk of Bootsy Collins, and, for old times' sake if nothing else, that hotel bar band, the Mustangs, with their no-pretensions good-time blast through Top-40 covers and golden-age oldies.

That in itself was not a conflict. Where he and Trey digressed violently was with Mike's fondness for, and desire to play, one of the few musical genres which hadn't impacted upon Trey, the bluegrass that lurks at the root of country music; that might, away from the good-ole-boy confines of the Grand Ole Opry and the Nashville cheese circuit, be termed real country music.

"It's the only context in which I feel patriotic," he would appeal when rehearsals broke down over the material he was introducing. "It's this country, and the people that live in the woods and the mountains of this country. It's a local thing, like macrobiotic people who only like to eat food from their region, it's the music of the country. . . . I just like the down-home attitude."

And that is what Trey objected to, the down-home shit-kicking image which adheres so stubbornly to bluegrass and country. For Trey, music was, and remains, a constant challenge, a process of growth through experiment and innovation. A band which is not forever trying to find fresh direction, to forge new links, might as well not be a band at all. For Mike, however, "It's more of a religious thing, and a meditation." In his mind, music was music, and it didn't matter whether you were the most original group in the world— never playing the same song twice, never even playing the same note twice—or the schleppiest bar band on the face of the earth, running down the Top 40 for a roomful of rednecks. So long as you were true to yourself, that was all that mattered.

"I'm on shaky ground when I talk about the philosophy of art," Mike concedes, "but . . . my main reason for doing this isn't artistic. I don't even consider myself an artist in the truest sense, because there are these things that supposedly make art high—originality; art being for art's sake; the fact that you can objectify it to be able to analyze it; and timelessness, the fact that it will stand the test of time. My favorite musical experiences are very timeful. They're just the moment." Mike could happily keep playing till the day he drops. Trey asserts that if he ever stopped wanting to try out new things, he would quit.

The clash of philosophies need not have been so violent. The psychedelic infusion which was already spinning Phish's first excursions into Trey's musical dream was deeply rooted in country traditions, via the Dead, of course, but also spiraling up through the influence of countless other musicians and combos. To Mike's way of thinking, names like Johnny Cash and Bill Monroe (who cut a rocking "Blue Moon of Kentucky" almost ten years before Elvis did) were as much a part of Phish's heritage as Duke Ellington and Charlie Parker. For example, Parker used to jam with Ray Price, one of the greatest honky-tonk singers of all, and to deny the unity which that alone personified was simply musical snobbery.

Reluctantly, begrudgingly, Trey nodded his acceptance. One of the things that kept him in Vermont was the chance to study under the composer Ernie Stires, a man whose entire philosophy was rooted in the belief, as Trey put it, that no matter how much you hate a certain style, if you can dig the music out of it and use it the way you want to use it, there's stuff to be learned. Trey hated bluegrass, but he wanted to learn. And today, Mike remains proud of his achievement. "Although Phish do play some of that stuff, we probably wouldn't if I hadn't started encouraging those guys to play some more of it."

Although all four band members certainly made their voices heard, Ernie Stires remains the single most powerful influence upon the nascent Phish. A jazz pianist working with the Vermont Symphony Orchestra, Stires was not in fact employed by the university. Indeed, UVM's music department did not even offer a course in composition to any students outside of the senior year, so Trey took his most important "classes" outside of the school curriculum, then passed them along to Phish in rehearsal.

Mike, learning later from Trey's own lessons, continued, "The way that Ernie writes, you hear a lot of dissonance, but there's a form to it. It's not just clashing notes because they clash. It's for a reason. It's to try to stretch certain limits and do it in a thoughtful way. So, for the listener, it's a matter of opening your mind to be able to accept that as being something desirable."

The composer Stravinsky said much the same thing: "Run from beauty and it will follow"; and it was from these two leads that Phish began their evolution, winding their way down the narrow pathway which divides the entertainer from the educator. In rehearsal, no matter how strongly they were divided by one another's personal tastes, the very fact that they could accept new ideas and learn from them was enough to justify the disagreements and fights. The knowledge that the music which ensued was utterly unclassifiable only added to their zeal.

"We just look at things from different angles," Mike argued. "The fact that we take opposite stances adds richness to the band."

It was that richness which would supplant the simplicity that lay at the heart of the Grateful Dead, in much the same way as the blues that fermented the older group's brew themselves had been supplanted since the hazy days of the Fillmore and the Avalon. Phish knew many of the traditions which the Dead once claimed for their own, but they met them several generations on, after those traditions had mutated through the power-chord creations of Cream and Jeff Beck, through the seventies rock of Led Zeppelin and AC/DC, through the prog-rock pastures of Argent and Yes. If the Dead were pioneers, striking out for virgin territory, Phish were the urban renewal squad, come to tear down the clichés and prop up the ruins.

That was what Mike found so inspiring, that bizarre blend of Ernie Stires out of early Yes, which made every rehearsal a fresh hurdle to clear. Bolstered, as well, by Fish's unflagging enthusiasm, and the knowledge that whatever they played, the pair of them really did work well together, Mike surrendered to the inevitable. He would rejoin Phish.

But before he did so, there were a few things he wanted to make clear. Trey wanted to take Phish deeper and deeper into self-composed musical territory. Mike agreed, but it would be a trade-off. For every couple of new songs, there would be a cover, something which the band could relax into; something, too, for the audience to hang on to, a safety net of sorts into which improvisation could fall if the occasion demanded. By the time Jeff Holdsworth added his voice to Mike's, Trey didn't really have an alternative.

Gigs became far more regular as Phish slipped back into the Burlington live scene. Partly that was the Dangerous Grapes' doing; people genuinely mourned their decision to quit, and a lot of fans transferred their affections to this strange-sounding new project. Trey's reputation helped the group out as well; it was no secret why he'd suffered his suspension, and with the spread of notoriety came a surge of curiosity. There were a lot worse ways to spend an evening than going to see a guy who sent a dead man's hand through the mail.

In November 1984, the band's confidence broadening with every new venue they found for themselves, and word of their talents spreading even farther afield, Phish landed their most prestigious gig yet. They were given a booking at Nectar's.

Nectarios "Nectar" Rorris began presenting local rock bands at his 188 Main Street bar and restaurant during the late 1970s. It was not the largest venue in town, holding maybe two hundred people at its sardine-can best, but the place boasted a cache which few others could match, a combination of long-standing tradition and impeccable taste. Before a group could play Nectar's, they needed to be special.

On December 1, 1984, little more than a year after their disastrous debut performance, Phish took the upstairs stage and gave the audience all they had. Opening the set with "Scarlet Begonias," they segued into Jimi Hendrix's "Fire," then moved deftly back to the Grateful Dead and "Fire on the Mountain."

A couple of original songs, "Slave to the Traffic Light" and "Makisupa Policeman," served notice of the direction Trey was moving Phish toward, Herb Alpert's "Spanish Flea" inducted a hint of light relief to the show, then "Skippy" and "Fluffhead" ended the night, with Steve Pollack appearing onstage out of nowhere, in full Dude of Life finery, to take over lead vocals.

And even though the four Phish originals were presented with little of the improvisational baggage which would eventually transform them into the epics they became, the band's enthusiasm, and the audience's support, was more than enough for Nectarios. He booked the group to return on the spot, and for the next three years, Nectar's would double as Phish's second home.

"When we played at Nectar's," Mike recalls, "it was so laid-back. We'd play three sets a night, just feeling our way as a band. It was such a mellow atmosphere that we were free to stretch out and experiment, to attempt outrageous things and make utter fools of ourselves."

Pretty soon, Phish weren't only playing three sets a night, they were playing three nights a week, and, literally, anything went.

Audiences who only knew of Trey as the guy who sent strange things through the post faded away; now it was people who'd heard about his band, the strange things they did, the odd songs they played. When the guitarist landed an early-morning DJ gig on the campus radio station, the *Ambient Alarm Clock Show*, that drew more people down to the bar. Now, hordes of fellow students were descending upon Nectar's, fully expecting, and often receiving, onstage performances which beggared belief.

"We were doing these plays onstage," remembers Trey, "trying out experimental, written-out, strange pieces of music, signing from that into hardcore stuff. It set our focus."

It also taught them never to be too self-judgmental. "We never really felt any pressure that we had to be good. All we had to do was have fun. We were going to be back the next two nights anyway. It taught us to take risks."

Musical risks were one thing, however; taking similar chances with one's education was quite another. Trey never forgave, or forgot, his suspension, and the closeted regimen of UVM was chafing Fish as well. Only Mike, preparing to switch his major from electronic engineering to film and communications, seemed content to see out his education there. Even before the opportunity presented itself, Fish and Trey were talking about transferring to a more enlightened university. And in Vermont, that meant only one place: Goddard College.

Located in Plainfield, in the wilds beyond Montpelier, the century-old Goddard had established itself among the country's most progressive colleges, a countercultural alternative that had forged its reputation in the wired white heat of sixties campus rebellion.

It had retained that spirit ever since. Goddard was distinguished by an almost totally open approach to its curriculum. No emphasis whatsoever was placed on grading: rather than being awarded A's, B's, or F's, students would be evaluated at the end of each semester according to their own personal merits. "In applying to Goddard," the college application form read, "you are invited to determine for yourself what kind of education is important to you, and whether the structures, freedoms and limits at this college will provide you with what you need. You are not asked to measure yourself against someone else's standards; you are not expected to fit a statistical profile of an imagined ideal student. We are concerned with you as you are, and as you hope to become." The concept of Top of the Class found no place at Goddard.

From its peak in the late 1960s, of course, the college's student population waned as dramatically as the Great Society it so fervently represented. The end of rebellion spelled the end of recruitment, and by the mid-1980s, Goddard was a utopian relic, a place where fewer than fifty students learned how not to become overachieving yuppie scumbags. In the world of Reaganomics, of Greed Is Good and Greed Is God, it shouldn't have stood a chance.

Nevertheless, it was popular on the live circuit, and Phish, whose fame was already leapfrogging the fifty miles from Burlington to Plainfield, were readily welcomed into Goddard's halls, both musically and socially. It was Mike's hallmate, Brian Long, who made the initial contact, recommending Phish for the annual Springfest show in April 1985. Springfest organizer Page McConnell was only one of the students eagerly awaiting them.

Born in Philadelphia on May 17, 1963, Page himself had arrived at Goddard only the previous fall. He transferred there to study musical improvisation from Southern Methodist University in Dallas, Texas. But his future career was mapped out long before he made that last, crucial transition.

Page's father, Jack, was one of the research scientists on the Johnson & Johnson teams that developed both Magnetic Resonance Imaging and Tylenol. Later, he would help found a health clinic on Hilton Head Island, South Carolina. What rubbed off on Page, though, was Jack's love of Dixieland jazz, and his skill on the banjo.

His mother, too, was a musician; she played mandolin, and as Page's own musical inclinations emerged, his parents felt no hesitation about encouraging them. By the time he hit high school, Page had already clocked up twelve years in his local, Basking Ridge, New Jersey, church choir, and thirteen years of piano lessons. Small wonder, then, that when he filled out his application to enroll at Lawrence Academy, a private school in Groton, Massachusetts, in September 1981, Page had listed only one favorite pastime: "Playing the piano. I love to make music."

Forty-five minutes outside of Boston on a good traffic day, close to the New Hampshire border and overlooking the rolling pastures of the sinisterly named Gibbet Hill farm, Lawrence was an excellent choice. Although academics is the school's main focus, there is also great emphasis placed on the arts, with gifted students allowed time both to work on, and excel in, these areas. Once ensconced at Lawrence, Page lost no time in throwing himself into the bustling musical curriculum, playing piano in a production of the play *Pal Joey*.

Moving into Sheedy Hall dormitory, directly above chemistry teacher Mr. Campolito's faculty apartment, Page spent most of his academic day in the single building that housed the school's auditorium, art rooms, and music rooms, working with the music teacher, Peter Hazzard. And though Page's career at Lawrence Academy was short, he remembers it with very fond clarity.

"I was only there one year, but it was certainly a memorable year, one of my favorite years in fact," he recalled in an interview with the academy's own eponymous magazine. "It was my first year away from home. I made a lot of good friends. I felt it was somehow a good place for me at that point." It was comforting, once he was settled at Goddard, to know Lake Groton was just a few miles down the road.

Page graduated from Lawrence in 1982. Penning his student's college recommendation, faculty member Joe Sheppard enthused, "What impresses me most about Page is that in spite of his broad popularity, he is very definitely his own person. He thinks independently, follows no fad, avoids fitting into any social mode, and has his values and priorities well thought out."

Watching Phish as they plowed confidently through a live set which evened out between covers and original material, Page brought all those qualities into play. The band impressed him: the tentative stabs at improvisation, the almost schizoid approach to their own songs and covers, the very fact that they refused to let conventional structure tie them down to one place. It was as if somebody was tapping into his own musical yearnings, and expanding them into an entire performance.

There was something missing, though: a melding of the group's formative ideas with the more concrete ground that a wider experience of music could bring them. As he watched Phish run through their set, Page could not shake the sense that they were pushing in directions which were already being stretched to their musical limits, but which could be twisted anew into something much fresher, if only the musicians would spread out a little farther. The show was barely over when Page was introducing himself; the introductions were barely over when he was pitching his own audacious vision to them.

The history of rock 'n' roll is strewn with chance meetings that went on to change the world. The day John Lennon met Paul McCartney has been considered important enough to have an entire book written about it, but there were countless other, equally crucial encounters: the morning when Mick Jagger bumped into Keith Richards on a packed commuter train; the evening Long John Baldry "discovered" Rod Stewart singing on a deserted railroad platform; the night Lou Reed met John Cale at a party in New York. . . .

The only moment that can compete with Page's arrival into Phish's life, perhaps, was that momentous evening when a red-haired, green-suited drunk lurched up to the band he'd been watching play, and told them, "I'm a better drummer than that geezer you've got." A few drinks later, a young Keith Moon joined an even younger Who.

But Page did not have to get drunk before he made his move, and he didn't push anyone else out of their job. They'd already heard what he could do on keys, playing in the R&B band that had appeared earlier in the show; besides, Phish themselves were already painfully aware that their sound desperately required some extra dimensions. The only thing they weren't sure about was where those dimensions would come from. With Trey ever keen to flaunt perceived wisdom and avoid the most obvious course at all costs, they toyed for a time with an extra percussionist, inducting Trey's Princeton Day School friend Marc Daubert just to see what would happen. It really didn't work.

Keyboards, on the other hand, probably would. Fleshing out the two guitars, weaving in between and under Trey's increasingly fluid solos, the instrument might well make all the difference. In May 1985 Page became a full-time member of Phish.

The five-piece Phish made their live debut that same month, at the Last Day Party on UVM's Redstone campus.

Page remained tentative, still finding his way through the morass of ideas which made up a "typical" Phish song, and the band's set that day offered only a hint of the changes which would soon be wrought: "McGrupp" and "Makisupa Policeman" still rubbed shoulders with the Grateful Dead covers, as "The Other One" made its way into the group's repertoire. Elsewhere, the Allman Brothers' epic "Whipping Post" offered Trey the opportunity to pull off some astonishing guitar pyrotechnics, confident that with Jeff and now Page filling in around him while Mike and Fish cemented the rhythm, Phish could expand like never before.

THE NEW ONES SUCK YOUR FACE RIGHT OFF

The arrival of summer vacation effectively returned Phish to the cocoon, as Trey and Fish headed off for a few weeks' busking around Europe. Phish were never far from their minds, however; by the time the pair returned, Trey had completed one new song, the effervescent "You Enjoy Myself," and was brimming with ideas for others.

Goddard College, too, continued to loom large in Phish's thoughts. Before they left Vermont for the summer, Trey and Fish both filed applications with the college, hoping to transfer into Goddard's Performing Arts program before the next semester began, in September 1985.

Not only was Goddard's approach to the field more open than any they ever encountered, but it also opened up a wealth of on-campus venues to Phish: the Haybarn Theater and the Music Building, of course, but as the college prospectus cheerfully put it, "performers find stages all over the campus." Page, incidentally, received a one-hundred-dollar headhunter's fee for his part in recruiting the pair of them.

Of course, Trey and Fish remained a familiar sight in Burlington. Three or four times a week, they joined Page in making the one-hundred-mile round-trip back to the city, strengthening Phish's hold on Nectar's and adding other bars to their itinerary: Finbar's, Hunt's . . . if there was a stage, Phish would fill it. At first, the group was recruited simply to open the show for better established Burlington bands like the Jones, and Lamb's Bread, but it was not long before the sheer enthusiasm of the Phish crowd propelled them to the top of the bill.

To catch Phish in the fall of 1985 as they expanded their geographical horizons and spread their musical wings was to see a band undergoing a vast transition—from uncertain art terrorists, trusting that other ears were open, to a band whose very attitude encouraged unyielding fidelity. Many of Phish's firmest fans today are people who first saw them play a decade ago; pushing thirty now, they can still recall the thrills which converted them in their teens.

Barb East caught Phish at Goddard in the fall of 1985. "I'd met this guy who lived on campus; if it wasn't our first date, it could only have been the second or third. I don't think he knew what he was inviting me to, it was just a dance, with live music, but it wasn't in one of the regular theater areas. It was in one of the classrooms, I think, or under one.

"Anyway, the band came on, and it was like they were playing a private party, and we'd just wandered in by mistake. They seemed to know everybody in the room except us, they were laughing and joking with people, taking requests, and they probably spent the first ten minutes just messing around up there.

"They were a very visual band. I don't think they were wearing anything out of the ordinary, but even when they were playing, there always seemed to be something going on, people pulling faces at each other, a lot of running around and jumping about. You felt they were trying to put each other off at times; Trey would be playing a solo, and Mike would just go over, stick his face into Trey's, it looked like he was licking Trey's nose at one point.

"What did they play? I recognized a couple of things; I think they played the theme from *Star Trek* at that one, and something by the Allmans, although I wouldn't swear to it. But I thought it was great, which was more than my date did; about halfway through, he asked if I wanted to go somewhere else, and when I told him no, I was enjoying myself, he just said, 'Suit yourself,' and fucked off. I don't think I ever saw him again. But I've seen Phish about a hundred times."

And every time would be different. Phish took their music seriously, but they did not extend that same pretension to themselves. One night, they would burn through an hourlong set without a word to each other, or a nod to the audience; another night, they would bounce onstage like a troupe of eager puppies, and reduce the room to hysterics without even glancing at their instruments. They could run through a set of covers like the best Top 40 bar band on the entire planet; or they lost themselves completely in a jam of critical complexity. Whatever, they were always in control, and if they felt like they weren't, if it suddenly seemed impossible to extricate themselves from a jam, one of them would always be there to concede defeat: "I'm sorry, but it really isn't going anywhere." Then the band would laugh, the crowd would join in, and someone would start playing "Spanish Flea" again.

Years later, discussing Phish's predilection for jamming, Mike admitted, "Standing onstage and playing music could be just like a nine-to-five job. It could be a boring routine if you let it." What Phish wanted to do was experience the reverse side of that syndrome, the unfettered freedom of playing a song for as long as they wanted, for as long as the other band members are up for it. "Remembering that sense of freedom is what makes it fun."

"A Phish jam is the ultimate abstraction," Trey believes. "Over time, the jams become more abstract. I've never really liked abstract music, [as] it doesn't seem to have any logic to it. I hope we can take people with us to a very abstract place, but one that's still connected to its grooves."

It was this connected abstraction which bled through the original songs which were now springing into Phish's live set.

Trey remained the group's most prodigious writer, and by the fall of 1985, "Alumni Blues," "Dog Log," and "Anarchy" were all firmly affixed within Phish's canon. There, they were joined by the purposefully obnoxious, but undeniably accurate, "Prep School Hippie," "Letter to Jimmy Page," and "Run Like an Antelope."

"Harry Hood" was another early favorite, all the more so since it immortalized a much-loved (or at least, much-noticed) local landmark, the giant Hood's Dairy billboard which stared unblinkingly through into the old red house which Trey shared with Page, Fish, and Brian Long, one of the most devoted of the Nectar's crowd. Every night, he would watch the company mascot, Harry Hood, disappear as the billboard lights went down, and he would just sit there and muse, "Harry, where do you go?" There was a song in there somewhere, and with a few helping lyrics from Brian Long, it didn't take Trey long to find it.

Despite his undeniable dominance, however, Trey showed at least a degree of egalitarianism by encouraging his fellows to challenge his position. Jeff's "Possum" was an immediate shoo-in; so was the unimaginatively titled but musically precocious "Mike's Song." And of course, when it came time to add fresh fruit to Phish's growing arsenal of crowd-pleasing covers, the floor was open to all comers, whether the band knew who they were or not.

A persistent voice in the audience one night might send

the band scurrying to learn the request; a chance conversation; a song on the radio; and, of course, the vast repository of favorites with which the musicians themselves grew up. From the Beatles' historic *White Album*, "Revolution" offered a foretaste of things to come. Trey's precious Allman Brothers remained a firm favorite, and "Revival" joined "Whipping Post" in the set. Bob Dylan's potentially raucous "Quinn the Eskimo" roared in to encourage a full-scale audience sing-along.

Later, Allen Toussaint's "Sneaking Sally Through the Alley" snuck out to remind people of the days when Robert Palmer was on the cutting edge of something more than Flash Harry videos. A full decade before "Addicted to Love" brought him the mass recognition he'd been deserving forever, the suave Englishman worked at the forefront of what the early 1970s' critics called blue-eyed soul—the same blue-eyed soul that David Bowie would mine for *Young Americans* and "Fame."

Phish's tastes were in a state of permanent flux, but there was one aspect of their repertoire that was not given new room to grow. They dropped the Dead from their stage show, and have never picked them back up since then.

Phish themselves had yet to get out of Vermont; not a word had been written, or a single song recorded. But in the corridors of campus, the whisper was already out: in Phish, the Dead met a tributary whose own pretensions were already tantamount to treason. Losing that group's songs from their now-swollen repertoire was only the first salvo Phish would fire against that pernicious rumor.

The group put its musical malleability down to the belief, as Fish put it, that "all music is conversation." Grimacing, he recalled how the group's earliest workouts were sometimes so disjointed that "we were all talking and no one was listening, which sounded horrible. Like Congress. So we started doing 'Hey!' exercises."

With the band members sitting in a circle, each would play a riff, a few bars, or a phrase, then wait while the rest joined in. The first person to realize everybody was playing perfectly in time would have to shout "Hey!" But if the shouter came in too early, it showed he was not paying attention, at which point his colleagues would administer a sound castigation. Fish admits that he was usually the one they caught out.

"We actually practice jamming exercises," Mike continued. "If a gig is good, it's always that we're hooked up as a unit and we're listening to each other and we're very aware. If it's ever a bad gig, it tends to be when different band members are in their own worlds and aren't aware of each other. So we do exercises in our practice room . . . to make sure that we can hook up and that each person can hear each band member and react to each other."

"The goal," Page concludes, "is to make sure you're listening, and to settle in as quickly as possible to the rhythmic or harmonic phrase." To this end, the group would often divide into pairs, one complementing the other, in counterpoint. An even more strenuous variation was to switch instruments. "The technique is not important here. It's the intention, what we're trying to do."

The result of this hard work is obvious every time Phish play together. "If we're jamming," says Mike, "it's possible that we'll suddenly change tempo to three times the speed, switch keys . . ." and rocket off on a whole different tangent. He will always treasure one description of Phish in full flight, "a herd of buffalos that were going fast through a field, and suddenly took a left turn together."

Their enthusiasm is infectious; so is their strength of purpose, a strength about which Mike is almost evangelical. And with good reason. In November 1985 the bassist underwent what he can describe only as an intense "religious experience," midway through a gig at the Goddard cafeteria. Over a decade later, Mike could still recall the moment, even if he was unable to spell out precisely what he felt.

"It was the peak experience of my life, the time I felt most myself. I knew I wanted to do this the rest of my life. Now I'm living to try to create and share the kind of experience I had in 1985." He told *Relix* magazine, "I've definitely grown since then, and I've learned how to achieve [different] levels of consciousness in music, and new musical levels since then. But I still consider that to be my peak experience. How transcendental it was."

It was this firsthand experience of the power of music that restoked Mike's belief in music as a meditative force—in stark contrast to Trey's studied artistry—that gave him the confidence to reinforce his position as the most outspoken member of the group, particularly when it was the group itself he was speaking out against.

Very early on in Phish's musical explorations, for example, it was Mike who stood firm against Page and Trey's attempts to chase new genres to their limits, always maintaining a strong grasp on the group's rock roots. He is still the loudest advocate of the unexpected, even unfamiliar, cover version; and he still looks somewhat awry on occasion, as when Fish occasionally steps out from behind his drum kit and starts to play the vacuum cleaner.

The vacuum cleaner was a joke the first time Fish played it; in fact, the drummer wasn't even sure that one could be played. He was at a friend's house-moving party when Page's girlfriend, Sophie Dilloff, asked him if he could play anything apart from the drums. Casting around the room, and spotting the vacuum in one corner of the room, Fish answered in the affirmative. He switched it on and put the nozzle to his mouth.

What happened next remains a highlight of the Phish live experience, all the more so since Fish learned how to truly manipulate the ensuing roars and raspberries. He speaks with the assurance of a true virtuoso: "There are fart sounds, Donald Duck sounds, and a blowing-across-a-bottle sound. If you get the spit caught in just the right place, you can get three or four tones bubbling at once." At the time, he was simply so overjoyed with the gurgling cacophony that he inserted the vacuum, a 1967 Electrolux, into Phish's very next concert.

But can the kids try this at home? Fish has never been sure of that, even after close to a decade spent playing the Electrolux, and a few nights watching his mother play it as well—Mimi Fishman has made a few guest appearances onstage alongside her son, proving that however complicated an instrument the vacuum may be, dexterity obviously runs in the family.

So he advises caution for anybody interested in having a go, caution and an eye for vintage models. He personally favors a 1956 model, claiming, "The new ones just suck your face right off. These old Electroluxes last forever, they never die, they have good motors." But, he worries, "I often picture myself as an old man, with one really long jowl on one side of my face and the other side totally normal." Which tends to be the moment when Trey cracks up, like the first time they met, saying, "Jon, you'll never look totally normal."

It was in an attempt to capture some of the formative magic which every new idea seemed to add to, that Phish set about recording their first "professional" demo tape, shortly before Christmas 1985. Taking over a four-track studio on the Goddard campus, Phish taped nine songs: "And So to Bed," "You Enjoy Myself," "Green Dolphin Street," "Harry Hood," "Slave to the Traffic Light," "Run Like an Antelope," "Divided Sky," and "Letter to Jimmy Page." With a live version of "Fluffhead" (featuring the Dude of Life on vocals) closing the collection, the tape was to become Phish's cold-calling card for the next year or more, mailed out to prospective club owners and booking agents as the band strove to broaden its horizons.

A more important body of work, however, was the catalog of songs which Trey intended to submit as his senior thesis—a conceptual body of work which he called *The Man Who Stepped into Yesterday*. Among Phish fans, it is better known as Gamehendge.

Although he would not deliver his thesis until the spring of 1988, elements of *The Man Who Stepped into Yesterday* were already appearing within Phish's repertoire; in fact, the seeds of this ambitious project were planted even earlier, by a poem which Tom Marshall wrote and mailed to Trey, called "McGrupp and the Watchful Hosemasters." Trey taped a copy of the poem to his dormitory door, and as early as May 1985 he was setting the poem to music. "McGrupp" was introduced into Phish's live set almost immediately.

A year later, another Tom Marshall composition, "Wilson," seemed to gel with the loose ideas suggested by "McGrupp." Slowly, a theme began to suggest itself, and Trey pursued it doggedly. By the time *The Man Who Stepped into Yesterday* was ready for its premier, in March 1988, all but two of its composite songs were already in-concert veterans.

Phish continued gigging locally into 1986, still building their reputation as a wild, free-form, and inventive aggregation; still sending audiences away bemused and bewildered, but convinced that whatever else Phish might be, they certainly weren't the sort of band you'd find playing any bar, Anytown.

New Hampshire fell to them, and Maine. They became comparative regulars on the downtown Portland, Maine, club scene, and began moving into Massachusetts.

According to Saul Penman, a Clarke University freshman in the spring of 1986, "Basically, there were only two groups which mattered; Phish, who came down from Vermont, and Blues Traveler, who would come up from New York. Other bands used to come and play, but most of them didn't matter. Whenever Phish or Blues Traveler came, though, it was like a huge band was playing. Even though they were only playing the little campus pub, everyone wanted to see them. The hippies would have big parties, and everyone else would run from the party to the show and back again all night."

Penman remembers some classic concerts. Anxious to recreate the Nectar's atmosphere in which they were nurtured, Phish took to playing two sets a night, at least when time allowed. "Sometimes, you got the impression they were just up there rehearsing. They'd be playing, stopping and starting, going back to the beginning of songs, all kinds of stuff you just weren't used to seeing bands do.

"The thing was, it never looked sloppy, or like they didn't care. It was more like they were breaking down the barriers between the band and the fans, the complete opposite to those big, slick, sterile shows which other bands were trying to do. And even when what they were playing went completely over your head, they still connected. I remember one night, Trey practically lectured us about fugues and atonal theory, the sort of stuff that only serious music students could even begin to understand, and you were standing there thinking, 'Oh my God, what's coming next . . . ?'—and then they played ZZ Top's 'Tush.' You just never knew what was going to happen next."

In the spring of 1986, just weeks beyond the end of the school year, and with Phish's date sheet already filling up with graduation and last-day dances, guitarist Jeff Holdsworth announced he was quitting the band.

With the benefit of hindsight, his decision was not too

surprising. Barb East remembers that of all the band members, Jeff was the one who held back the most when the stage show grew anarchic and the jokes flew faster than the riffs and chords. His bandmates, too, knew something was amiss. Jeff's commitment to Phish was never doubted, but the amount of sacrifice he was prepared to make was open to question, by Jeff if not by his colleagues. A recently born-again Christian, he was accustomed to living a very different life than his fellows. But he wanted to play very different music as well, to sing the praises of something a little more profound than antelopes, possums, and milkmen.

More important, however, was Jeff's knowledge that he would not be remaining in Burlington after graduation as an electrical engineer in May. He was heading back to his home state, New Jersey, to put his qualifications to good use (and, contrary to oft-stated rumors, he never did join a band with Jimmy Swaggart!).

Jeff's departure was both amicable and instructive. It showed his erstwhile bandmates that no matter what else is going on in your life, you must always follow your own convictions. Such personal integrity has yet to be recognized as a bona fide religion, but still it is a pathway from which Phish have tried desperately hard not to stray.

For a very brief moment, Phish did consider casting around for a replacement for Jeff. Much of their set, after all, was arranged for five instruments, with some of Trey's most treasured solos based around the knowledge that there was another guitar to take up any slack. That they ultimately opted not to replace him, that they coupled that with a refusal to substantially rework their live show, only emphasizes the self-confidence the band now possessed.

Once past their first rehearsal as a four-piece, when every song seemed to have a gaping hole where the rhythm used to play, the very challenge of circumventing those gaps seemed to add to the strength of the music. Sequences that once were as familiar as a walk down Main Street, now became tests of agility and endurance.

Page, in particular, relished these newfound freedoms. Remembering the things that most attracted him to Phish in the first place, but aware that many had yet to bear fruit, Page grasped this brief moment of musical flux with the evangelical fervor of a Bible Belt preacher.

Page brought more than a distinctive keyboard sound to Phish, though. He was also accompanied by a long-standing love of jazz, inherited from his father, of course, but honed to perfection by his own relentless curiosity. From Art Tatum and Thelonius Monk, to Joey DeFrancesco and Jimmy Smith, Page's tastes ran the gamut of styles, and he knew that Trey was alert to at least some of those influences. Now it was time to transform that alertness into action.

"Page was pretty excited about jazz from the beginning," Trey recalled, "and he started to push us to do these jazz gigs." But he also admits that not much pushing was required. Under the all-encompassing eye of his tutor, Ernie Stires, Trey himself began studying big-band jazz. Winning Fish and Mike over to the possibilities of the new discipline was the next step, and soon, Phish were moonlighting from their own career with regular Monday-night gigs backing horn players in a whole new quarter of Burlington's club world. "Slowly, over time," Trey sums up, "we started picking up on the jazz thing."

Every week, the group would transform itself into the Johnny B. Fishman Jazz Ensemble, recruit a horn section and play the cafes—as Mike says, "Just to try and learn some things from the horn players." Offstage, the four musicians exhausted every local repository of archive jazz, live and recorded; in rehearsal, they would set themselves the almost impossible targets of learning the style of eras gone by. (Years

later, in 1994, Phish would take a similar crash course in bluegrass.)

As Trey remains at pains to point out, "Jazz is really an
important thing to learn, on a lot of different levels. Harmon-
ically and musically, you learn so much from jazz, even if
you're not going to be a straight-ahead jazz player. Any kind
of musician can learn from jazz."

Phish's attempts to immerse themselves in the music
didn't always work; in fact, they rarely ever came off with total
success. According to Mike, what usually developed was a
sound which owed its genesis to rock 'n' roll, "but some of
the ideas of improvisation might come from jazz." And that
was what mattered most: the fact that even if they could never
play the music firsthand, Phish were absorbing enough of it
so that when it did emerge, in a song or a sequence, it would
sound like it belonged there—and not stick out like a badly
placed wart.

Too many bands had tumbled into that trap already, and
as the 1980s rushed toward their midpoint, many more
seemed destined to join them, tumbling headlong into the
depths of dilettantism as rock sought to rediscover the smug
self-importance it enjoyed before the firestorms of punk rock.
More than ever before, the dustbin of oblivion yawned hun-
grily open, and it only took one false note to pitch the unwary
into it. If Phish intended to be clever, they needed to stay
smart as well. In years to come, as their fame spread and the
inevitable detractors became more analytical in their attacks,
it was that smartness which would give Phish the strength
they would need to survive.

The slowly increasing canon of live recordings, the first
tapes made by friends (but rapidly spreading far beyond that
immediate circle), provides the strongest evidence of the
speed with which the group's horizons were expanding. An
October 1985 Finbar's tape, for example, includes the loping

"Camel Walk," the increasingly convoluted "Mike's Song," and a song which might well represent Phish at the height of their early, interpretive powers, a rendering of King Crimson's "Discipline" which has become so powerfully individual as to be all but unrecognizable. Indeed, long-term Phish tapers probably know it better as "Dave's Energy Guide."

The only thing that unites these songs is the absolute absence of unity. Phish sloughed moods like other people change clothes, slipping effortlessly from grinning inanity to studious pomposity, then exploring the middle ground at their leisure later on. It was as if they were daring their audience to categorize them, and though they would sometimes pause long enough to at least inspect what people were saying, it was only so they could skew off somewhere else within moments.

It was in between these increasingly wide-ranging journeys, with Page at the wheel of the band's old van, that Phish began piecing together a new demo tape, one which would hopefully offer a more representative study of their capabilities—individual and collective—than the increasingly outdated demo they were still mailing around.

Retaining several songs from the earlier tape, this latest batch of recordings (known to fans, with what would one day prove confusing prescience, as the *"White Album"*) was not, in fact, a full Phish recording. The band as a whole appeared on only a handful of songs; rather, the tape compiled demos recorded separately by Trey and Mike, with Trey's contributions moving relentlessly toward his eventual *The Man Who Stepped into Yesterday* goal, as another future Gamehendge song, "AC/DC Bag," slips in midway through.

Other Anastasio favorites, "Run Like an Antelope" and "Alumni Blues," "Divided Sky" and "Dog Log," rub shoulders with what are often mere fragments of songs and ideas:

"Aftermath," "Ingest," "Hamburger," an ode to nitrous oxide, "B:N20," and the delightfully titled "Fuck Your Face."

The end result is both confused and confusing; from an historical point of view, the *White Album* is best regarded as a reminder of just how far removed from one another Trey's and Mike's musical tastes ran. For it shows, in that removal, a great deal of the common ground which has kept their relationship intact. Left to their own musical devices, the pair could tear Phish asunder. Accepting the need for compromise as they do, they are the glue that not only binds the band together, but provides a bond with their audience, too. Few Phish fans can honestly claim they have adored everything the band has ever done. Knowing that either Mike or Trey would agree with them makes admitting that fact an awful lot easier.

Phish's relationship with their audience, however, went a lot deeper than merely a common empathy. Even today, Trey reckons, "I [can] look down on the front row and I can probably name or recognize a third of the people there. It's weird, I feel like I'm playing in a roomful of buddies." In 1986–87, that feeling was even stronger: "We always knew everybody in the audience." It was only natural, then, that as the band's popularity grew, and with it the need to delegate certain non-musical responsibilities, Phish should hand-pick their assistants from the crowd on the dance floor.

Paul Languedoc had been a familiar face on the Phish scene ever since Trey wandered into Time Guitars, where Paul was then working, to have some customized work done on one of his own guitars. A luthier by trade, Languedoc built his first guitar when he was eighteen, and by the time he met Trey, he had several hundred instruments to his credit, beautifully crafted and inlaid guitars, each one absolutely unique.

Certainly it was that talent which initially attracted Trey, but the two struck up an immediate friendship, which quickly spilled over into the group. Within a matter of weeks, Paul took over Phish's bookkeeping duties from Mike; he was there to help the group load in before shows, and to pack up at the end. He began working with both Trey and Mike, designing instruments for them. And when they needed someone to work the soundboard for them, at Hunt's in Burlington on October 15, Paul was up for that job as well.

It was amazing how much difference a full-time engineer could make when compared to the fill-in friends and disinterested strangers who normally twiddled the knobs for the band. Maybe it wasn't the first time Phish sounded like a real, professional beat combo; it was, however, the first time they realized just how good they were capable of sounding. On the spot, Paul was offered a permanent job behind the soundboard. He still holds that position today.

He arrived just in time to see Phish make their first journey out of New England, for a show at Penn State University. They traveled down there expecting the worst—and they got it. Even the excited word-of-mouth which sustained Phish in the northeastern states could only travel so far, so fast. They arrived at the gig to find the room almost empty, and it remained that way throughout their performance.

"Hey! We're Phish!" Fish shouted into the silent darkness. "Are you ready to rock 'n' roll?" Trey bellowed to himself. And though the band played a dynamite show, laced with all the favorites, tapes of the gig have a deep, eerie resonance, the sound of a great group playing with itself.

Back home, of course, the madness showed no signs of subsiding. Shows at Nectar's, once the province of a handful of fans and a clutch of baffled onlookers, were now little short of anarchy—frenetic, full, and a free-for-all. Once a month, from Sunday through Thursday, Phish would make Nectar's their own, watching as regulars vied to outdo one another in their knowledge of the songs and their relationships with the band, an elaborate game of one-upmanship designed to keep the gradual intake of newcomers in their place.

It was all very friendly, and jocular too, but it was significant nevertheless, indelibly branding the band as one which inspired fervent loyalty, and establishing within that fervency the sense that Phish and fan alike were in this business for the long haul. For outsiders curiously gazing in, the old observation of a manic private party remained the only point of reference that made any sense.

"We were horrible," Barb East reflects. "I wasn't even part of the inner sanctum; that was people like Amy Skelton and Brian Long, the ones who'd been around since the beginning, and it was like they formed a protective cordon around the band. Then around them, there would be another circle, and surrounding them another one, all the way to the back, which is where the first-timers would stand, sort of paying their dues.

"You could tell who they were, as well. There was one night, just before Christmas [1986], some guy was at the back, and he obviously didn't have a clue, but he wanted to make like he did. Right at the beginning of the show, some people were calling out for 'David Bowie,' and the band played it really early on. This one guy, though, he'd got caught up in the shouting, and for the rest of the night, that was all he did, shouted out for 'David Bowie,' completely unaware that the band had played it, and that the rest of us were now shouting it simply to wind him up. By the end of the set, even Trey had shouted it out once or twice!"

"David Bowie" was one of the newest songs in Phish's set, but it rose quickly to the forefront of the fans' choice of favorites. Written by Trey in honor of the former Ziggy Stardust's forthcoming birthday, this sharp piece of wordplay featured just one lyric, the simple juxtaposition of Bowie's name with that of the British band UB40. Within that juxtaposition, however, there lurked a very witty pun, and Bowie, for whom forty was a milestone which he greeted from his weakest commercial position in years, probably wouldn't have thanked Phish for delivering it.

Phish's onstage spontaneity, at Nectar's and elsewhere, their readiness to answer audience requests, may have been confusing to new fans, but to older hands, it was simply another illustration of their inherent strength, the confidence by which each member was sustained. Then as now, pre-gig set lists were compiled as rough guides only, "in case we run out of ideas," Trey smirked; in their stead, Phish would literally go wherever the music took them, telegraphing their ideas to one another with a word—sometimes no more than a nod—before they raced into audacious, fresh territory.

Chris Kuroda, a Phish fan long before he became their full-time lighting technician, explained, "On occasions, the band writes set lists. [But] a lot of times, they write what are called reference sheets, thirty songs on a piece of paper, and they might do any one of these." Or they might not.

At other times, Phish would take the stage with a fully regimented set list, painstakingly compiled while they waited to go on. Kuroda continued. "They will literally sit there for an hour and a half and formulate a set list, think about it, how they want the show to go, what would go good after this. Then they'll walk onstage and they won't play a single tune [off it], not one. They won't even open with the first song, so it's pointless." Instead, they would simply tap in to the audience's mood, whether introspective, extroverted, content just to sit, or eager to dance—and take it to the limit.

Stevie Wonder's extravagant funk fest "Boogie On, Reggae Woman" was no stranger to their early set, neither was the Who's rocking "Sparks." And either could find itself rubbing shoulders with the spiritual "Swing Low, Sweet

Chariots" on the one hand, Lynyrd Skynyrd's soaring "Free Bird" on the other.

Another popular inclusion in Phish's set was Frank Zappa's "Peaches en Regalia." This most overt reference to the composer and musician whose art hangs so heavily over Phish's own has, strangely, passed many of the band's greatest critics by. That same popular, insular thought, which flagged Phish as just one of so many Dead tribute outfits, continued along its mistaken way long after any original truth became utterly blurred by reality.

It was Zappa, for instance, whose lead Phish were following when they began practicing and rehearsing their improvisations. As all four band members have pointed out over the years, the Grateful Dead never, ever did that, but Zappa advocated it all the way through his career. "The project/object," as Zappa detailed it, "contains plans and non-plans, also precisely calculated event-structures designed to accommodate the mechanics of fate and all bonus statistical improbabilities attendant thereto. . . . [It] incorporates any available visual medium, consciousness of all participants (including audience), all perceptual deficiencies, God (as energy) . . . and other things." Or, in other words, not even his accidents were accidental.

David Walley, author of the Zappa biography *No Commercial Potential*, continues. "Each [Zappa] album, each concert, had its own particular function. There was purpose to each lyric, melody, arrangement, improvisation, tune sequence, choice of material." And while he concedes that only someone who had attended every single one of Zappa's recording sessions, rehearsals, and concerts "could become aware of the whole of the work" (which in turn meant only Zappa himself), still the point is apparent. Even when he appeared to be verging on the anarchic, Zappa always knew what he was doing.

Phish shared that sense of purpose, echoed it in their use of lyrics as a landscape around which the music would entwine, and song titles which suggested themes, but never dictated them. "In a twenty-minute song which has five words," Mike insisted, "those five words are much more meaningful than some with a hundred words."

By those standards, many of the criticisms which would be aimed at Phish as their career progressed were already secondhand: Zappa, too, was accused of pointless flippancy, of meaningless lyrics, of indulgent chicanery. The inclusion of "Peaches en Regalia" in Phish's live set was their way of acknowledging their debt to Zappa, at the same time as offering the raised fist of solidarity. The addition, in 1988, of "Big Leg Emma," Zappa and the Mothers of Invention's first-ever 45, seconded that emotion.

Yet it cannot be denied that there was also a very real sense of pop dilettantism to Phish's burgeoning catalog of covers; a foreboding belief that songs were introduced to the set not because the band needed to play them, but because they had just discovered them for themselves, and were now out to prove just how broad their tastes, and their talents, really were.

"She's Got the Katy" and "Corinna," for example, were drawn from the Taj Mahal songbook—a reminder of the days, at the twilight of the 1960s, when the bluesman was widely regarded as a potential mainstream attraction—but were also a gesture of profound arcanity. Who, after all, listened to Taj Mahal in the eighties?

Long-term critical favorites like Jimi Hendrix, Earl Scruggs, and Little Feat were frequent visitors to the set list, but it was easy to question Phish's real motives: An honest tribute, and a crowd-pleasing diversion? Or an excuse to match their own abilities against those of such incontrovertible masters? Even such contemporary references as America's Talking Heads ("Cities") and Britain's XTC ("Melt the Guns") were open to suspicion; once again, both were bands whose musical dexterity, and eccentricity, placed them far beyond the traditional confines of rock 'n' roll.

The corollary to all this, of course, was the sheer delight with which Phish would, and could, assail such traditional classic rock chest-beaters as Led Zeppelin's anthemic "Good Times Bad Times," the James Gang's "Walk Away," and ZZ Top's "Tush." On occasions such as these, Phish would drop all their defenses, discard their pretensions, and simply blast away like the good ole bar band they never, ever, wanted to become.

And if their take on Edgar Winter's "Frankenstein" never eclipsed the performance Winter himself trotted out for an oft-bootlegged British television show one memorable night in 1973, Phish have breathed such fresh life into that monster that almost ten years on from its in-concert debut, it was still turning up in their repertoire occasionally.

THEY'RE NOT OUR BAND ANYMORE

On August 21, 1987, Phish journeyed down to Hebron, New York, where they were invited to play at a friend's barbecue party. Hosted by farm owner Ian McClain, this open-air show is one of the most fondly remembered of all Phish's eighties shows, not only for the sheer quality, and durability, of their show that day, but also for the air of rustic ease which permeated the concert site.

Refreshments of every imaginable kind were available, as every concertgoer, it seemed, brought their own contribution to the forthcoming feast—but what stayed longest in most people's minds was the sheer number of dogs in attendance that day, and the absolute cacophony of barking which accompanied every song. The sole consolation for any tapers in the audience was that Marley, Trey's eighteen-month-old golden retriever, was the only hound within reach of a microphone. Phish's newly elected Head of Security spent the entire show onstage, watching her master.

Phish themselves got into the spirit of the event with three sets rich in canine imagery: "Dog Log" opened, "Funky Bitch," "Shaggy Dog," "Harpua," and "McGrupp" were all taken out for a walk onstage. Then there was "Divided Sky," whose melody Trey lifted from one of his mother's songs for children, "Gus the Christmas Dog." And at least one review of the show, published in the fans' guide *The Pharmer's Almanac*, described the gig from a dog's point of view. "What a great tail-wagging time I had!"

Before returning to school, Phish played at least one other outdoor show that summer, at the Mead Ranch in Shelburne, a farming town five miles south of Burlington. They continued to work the local barroom circuit through September. It was in the midst of all this activity that Trey continued leading the band into the realms of Gamehendge.

In the year since he had begun working seriously on the project, *The Man Who Stepped into Yesterday* had developed from a clutch of vaguely related songs into a vast yet reasonably self-contained allegorical fairy tale. It advanced, too, from a simple musical exercise into the body of work he intended to present as his Senior Study.

In accordance with Goddard's own specifications, it was already approved by the lead faculty member of the campus program. A faculty adviser and a so-called Second Reader had agreed to supervise and evaluate the project as it moved toward completion. As Trey's final year before his proposed graduation passed by, few Phish shows took place that did not feature at least one, and often several, of the songs Trey earmarked for *The Man Who Stepped into Yesterday*. Not only was it important to hone the songs as close to perfect as they could, they also worked in the knowledge that one of Trey's academic peers might also be present, checking up on his progress.

Drawing upon, and parodying, everything from organized religion to the white man's colonization of the Americas, *The Man Who Stepped into Yesterday* was set in the mythical land of Gamehendge, and detailed the cultural collision of modern man, in the guise of a traveler named Wilson, and the Lizards, a race of primitive people indigenous to that world.

Of course, the story was deliberately analogous with the first contact between Europeans and Native Americans; later in the cycle, Wilson's subjugation of the Lizards, and his theft of their Bible, the Helping Friendly Book, produced further similar, if clumsy, parallels. Saul Penman admits that elements of the story "always made me think of the Doors, with Morrison as the Lizard King and his never-ending journey," although an equally plausible comparison allies *The Man Who Stepped into Yesterday* with C. S. Lewis's classic children's novel, *The Lion, the Witch, and the Wardrobe*. (A decade later, Trey and Tom Marshall would at least partially remark upon this with a new song, "Prince Caspian," titled for another of Lewis's fantasies in the Chronicles of Narnia.)

In Lewis's tale, three children enter a large antique wardrobe and find themselves in the fabled land of Narnia; Trey's protagonist, a washed-up military veteran named Colonel Forbin, also enters through a door. Lewis's children discovered wonderment and adventure, Forbin discovers fresh meaning to an hitherto empty life. The children defeat an evil Queen and save Narnia; Forbin defeats an evil King (Wilson) and retrieves the Helping Friendly Book. And, just as the victorious children are elevated to Royal status, Forbin is raised to godhood.

Around these principal characters and events, a host of lesser figures populate the story: an electronic hangman which Wilson calls the AC/DC Bag; Icculus, the Lizards' own god, and his sidekick the Famous Mockingbird; McGrupp, Forbin's pet dog; Rutherford the Brave, the Sloth, Tela, and Errand Wolfe; the revolutionaries fighting against Wilson's despotic regime; and so on. It is these characters around whom the musical's eight songs revolve.

The story is not the most original ever devised, but Trey

did draw from sources far and wide for his characters' names and attributes. Inasmuch as both flew too close to the sun, literally in one instance, figuratively in the other, Icculus was surely derived from the Greek legend of Icarus. "Rutherford the Brave" could have been named for the bass player with Genesis, while "McGrupp" certainly shared more than four letters of his name with McGruff, the trenchcoat-clad canine adopted as the mascot of the 1970s' TV Crime Awareness project.

Of course, Trey was not being judged according to the originality of his story, and on March 12, 1988, *The Man Who Stepped into Yesterday* was debuted live at Nectar's. Although only two of its composite parts, "Tela" and "Colonel Forbin's Ascent," had never previously been performed live, songs that had hitherto been performed in isolation were finally aired in their intended form, linked by the sometimes lengthy (but in this arena, seldom boring) narrative which Phish accompanied by gentle jamming.

Two months later, Trey delivered Phish's studio recreation of the same performance to his faculty adviser, and at the end of May 1988 (one year after Page underwent the same tense ritual, graduating with a Senior Study called *The Art of Improvisation*), Trey took his place alongside his fellow seniors at Commencement.

None of them knew what their fate was. Graduation, like so much else at Goddard, was a communal affair, and as nonjudgmental as it could possibly be. Each senior would be handed a large envelope, to take from the rostrum and open at their leisure. If their account with the school was settled— their tuition fees paid, reports delivered on time, and their Senior Study completed and accepted—the envelope would contain their diploma. If anything was lacking, it would contain a letter outlining the outstanding requirements.

Trey tore the package open. He'd made it.

The fact that Trey would graduate on schedule indicates that academic success is reliant upon very different, and doubtless more worthwhile, indices than rock 'n' roll criticism. But though *The Man Who Stepped into Yesterday* was undoubtedly impressive on certain levels, it remains a somewhat flawed, not to mention immature, piece of work.

The reliance upon narration as a link between (and during) songs continues to betray the fact that the concept itself was not strong enough to sustain its obvious ambition. Yet it is also true that the handful of live performances which Phish have, over the years, devoted to the saga, have seen many of its original musical weaknesses ironed out, and elements of *The Man Who Stepped into Yesterday* have not only endured, they have grown with retelling.

The *Rocky Horror*–esque "AC/DC Bag," "The Sloth," "Famous Mockingbird," and Jeff Holdsworth's "Oh! Possum" have all become comparative regulars in Phish's live repertoire.

In addition, Trey maintained his own interest in the saga with occasional appendages to it. A title track, which Phish first performed in 1987, but which was omitted from the final work, 1989's "Punch Me In The Eye" (as Trey calls the song; tapers have immortalized it as "Punch You In The Eye") and the 1990 composition "Llama" have done much to lighten the load of the cycle. It was, Trey, Page, and Fish concurred, only a matter of time before Phish recorded a full Gamehendge album. All they needed to do was convince Mike to go along with it.

He was going to take a lot of convincing. "There are some good songs, [but] . . . the whole 'story' aspect of it has never been my thing. Maybe we would have done it already, if I hadn't been negative about it before."

Yet the obvious affection with which Phish fans regard this earliest example of the band's inventiveness notwithstanding, his negativity is not only understandable, it can perhaps be applauded.

Publication of *The Man Who Stepped into Yesterday*, in anything like its original form, would have done no more favors to Trey (and by extension, the band) than the unearthing of Stephen King's high school essays could do for him. Youthful strivings and ambition are great, but not if one wishes to keep growing in that field.

Trey himself acknowledged this in 1996, driving the final nail into Gamehendge's coffin when he canceled the production of a proposed CD-ROM. "We've never made any money off Gamehendge," he told *Musician*, "and that's what's kept it a cool thing. We made a vow that we will never make money off any of those songs. So we canceled the CD-ROM."

Even as Trey sweated to complete *The Man Who Stepped into Yesterday*, through the spring of 1988, Phish continued playing live around town. In April, they even put themselves up against such local talents as the Hollywood Indians and Screaming Broccoli in a Battle of the Bands at the Front, and ran out easy victors. The following month, Phish celebrated Trey's graduation by inviting Page's old tutor, Karl Boyle, to blow sax with them onstage when they played the Goddard Springfest.

All four band members had by now made Burlington their home, a base they shared with their burgeoning support team: Amy Skelton, official First Fan and the grandiloquently titled Merchandising Manager who sold home made T-shirts and tapes at each show; Paul Languedoc, soundman and guitar technician; Jim Pollock, a fellow Goddard student and a talented cartoonist who was quickly pressganged into designing the band's merchandising; Nancy Taube, who would write the early Phish favorites "I Didn't Know" and "Halley's Comet"; Tim Rogers, who would flit between the lighting board and the stage, where he added occasional harmonica to the stew; and the host of willing hands who passed through the rank of roadie.

The network was expanding, as well. Almost every time Phish played out of town, they met somebody else who could help them in some way, whether it was simply networking with friends to ensure ever-larger turnouts, or a more tangible offer of new venues to work.

Despite all this, there were still gaps even in Phish's New England itinerary, which is what brought John Paluska to Burlington.

A student at Amherst College in western Massachusetts, Paluska became intrigued by Phish long before he ever saw them play. One of his friends, Mike Billington, had recently moved up to Burlington with his own outfit, Ninja Custodian, and was already raving about the group. Other friends, too, were confirmed fans of the band, and when they announced they intended spending Spring Break '88 in the mountains of Vermont, dividing their time between the slopes and some Phish shows, Paluska did not need to be asked twice. And once he'd seen the group in action, he was hooked.

Talking to Phish afterward, of course, he could not resist asking them why he'd been forced to haul himself up to Vermont to see them play; most bands, after all, took themselves on the road, and met their fans on their home turf.

The band's reply was simple. They'd never played Amherst because they'd never been asked to. Three weeks later, Paluska offered Phish their first-ever paying engagement outside of Vermont. He booked them to play Humphries House, the on-campus home of the Zoo cooperative theme house and theater where he happened to be Social Director. It took its name, of course, from UMass's own nickname.

He followed that by landing Phish further shows at the University of Massachusetts and at the neighboring Hampshire College, then began reaching farther afield, to Pearl Street, the premier off-campus bar in Northampton. And Paluska's convictions seemed somehow contagious. Within weeks of their first Zoo gig, Phish scored a similarly lucrative show across the state line in New Hampshire, at the Steak House in the tourist haven of Squam Lake. And shortly after that, the group was invited to undertake the biggest road trip of their life, for a week of shows in Telluride, Colorado.

Burlington seemed to sense Phish's growing national profile. There was not a bar in town which they could not now fill, even during the summer, when most of the college crowd had long since flown south. Certainly they had outgrown Nectar's; gigs there were so packed that Phish were actually becoming bad for business, as people simply gave up trying to fight their way to the bars and the waitresses surrendered any dreams they'd once harbored of finding a path through the crowd to the diners.

In July, with a new residency already arranged with the Front, Phish announced they were leaving Nectar's forever. On July 25, 1988, Phish played their final show at the club which had done so much to sustain and support them, a packed and somewhat tearful farewell that drew upon every live favorite with which they'd ever regaled that audience. Surveying the solid mass of humanity swaying in front of the stage, it was plain that Phish really were on the move.

A week later, they were on the road to Colorado—which was when they discovered that their original booking was canceled. They plowed on regardless, confident that the friends who'd won them the original shows would sort something out when they got there.

Even by Vermont standards, the Moon was a tiny club. In truth, Telluride itself is scarcely much more than an ink spot on most maps of the state. Perched on the western slopes of the Rocky Mountains, where the Red Mountain, Pass carries travelers a breathtaking 11,000 feet above sea level, the town was founded on the mining industry, which sustained so much of Colorado's early wealth; in fact, the town was named for its principle mineral source, the metal Tellurium.

Voracious mining long ago devoured what was, as recently as 1950, still regarded as the city's principle industry, and were it not for an equally aggressive approach to tourism, Telluride might well have fallen off the map altogether, or disappeared into the kind of crumbling, ghost-ridden half-life which Cripple Creek and Victor then labored beneath. Now, however, it was booming again, a year-round ski resort with an appetite for live entertainment.

That first night at the Moon, the largely college-age crowd simply ate up Phish. They came back for more the next night as well. It was the same story at the Roma, where Phish played in exchange for a percentage of the door receipts.

Even more importantly, when those people went home— or back to school in the fall—they carried word of Phish in their luggage; some even carried rough tapes which they'd made, copied, or bought. Visitors from elsewhere around Colorado itself appear to have been especially vocal; it would be almost two years before Phish returned there, and maybe it really is (as one Denver fan puts it) down to a local surfeit of ski bums, but Colorado remains one of the most loyal Phish strongholds in the entire United States.

Phish returned to Burlington in triumph; launched their residency at the Front in majestic splendor. But not everybody, it seemed, was happy with the way things were going. One night as he was passing through the crowd, Mike heard for the first time the plaintive observation which would become a veritable mantra as Phish's popularity increased.

A woman at the bar sounded almost tearful as she loudly

complained, to anyone who would listen, and a few hundred more, "They're just not our band anymore."

Regular gigs in and around Vermont were now supplemented by almost equally regular trips across the border into Maine, New Hampshire, New York, and Massachusetts. Most of their out-of-state shows were colleges: Clark University in Worcester, Massachusetts, remained a popular haunt; so did Hamilton College in Clinton, New York, where Phish celebrated Halloween with a storming set and a wild costume party. John Paluska, out in Amherst, was bringing in shows on a more-than-monthly basis, while back home, both the UVM and Goddard welcomed its distinguished alumni back with undisguised zeal.

If any show could be described as more important than all those others, however, it was that night in early November when the group crossed the Boston city limits for the first time in anger, and set up shop at a bar called Molly's, on Brighton Avenue, Allston.

The bar was popular with the Boston University crowd; it was, in fact, a BU student, Ben "Junta" Hunter, who rented the bar for Phish in the first place, and then wallpapered the campus with handbills and posters. It was only small, and the turnout for the show wasn't much bigger. But from the moment the audience returned to their dorms and started raving about the evening they'd spent, Junta Hunter was under constant siege from people who wanted to find out what they'd missed. The next day he was back at Molly's, rebooking the bar for a night in December. And this time, the place was packed. If Boston really is the Holy Grail for New England club bands, Phish had enjoyed a serious taste of the treasures it contained. Now they wanted to dive in there with them.

Earlier in the year, Phish had finally got around to updating their demo tape, ducking into Euphoria Studios in the Boston suburb of Revere to record a handful of songs. It was an impressive effort; working for the first time with a professional engineer, the studio's own Gordon Hookaloo, Phish came closer to nailing their in-concert spontaneity than even they'd expected. But though the tape was certainly instrumental in landing them a number of new venues, Molly's included, few big-time Boston promoters paid them any heed. Any local reputation Phish possessed remained tightly confined to excited reports about this weird provincial group who got the college kids going; so far as Beantown's hard-bitten seen-it-all, done-it-all entrepreneurs were concerned, there was nothing either on the grapevine or on the tape to interest a wider audience.

Junta Hunter added his weight and the door receipts from Molly's to their résumé, but there were no takers. Phish, however, were not going to take apathy for an answer. Pooling their own resources, scraping together every cent they could, Junta Hunter and John Paluska decided to book, and promote, a mainstream Boston show for themselves.

It was a courageous move, all the more so since the venue they selected, the Paradise, on Commonwealth Avenue, was widely regarded as among the most important, and certainly the most public, clubs in the city. U2, the Psychedelic Furs, Billy Bragg, and the Lords of the New Church all commenced their individual conquests of America at the Paradise, and while a successful show at the venue, under the watchful eye of promoter Don Law, might not necessarily make a band, an unsuccessful one would almost unquestionably break them.

For weeks before the January 26, 1989, show, Phish circulated news of their audacity among their fan base. They didn't expect too many people to follow them down from Vermont, but with so much of the band's capital, not to mention reputation, riding on the showcase, every head would help.

The first sign of something going seriously right came as

Phish parked their van outside the club. Comm Ave was already seething with people, most of whom, Phish suddenly realized, they either knew or at least recognized. Every third car, and certainly a couple of buses, seemed to have Vermont license plates.

The club bouncers, less observant, maybe, and certainly less than interested, headed to their work stations that evening looking forward to an easy night. Nobody, least of all the club's owners, expected anything out of the ordinary from the night's entertainers; a handful of stragglers, some friends of the band, it was the next-best thing to a full night off.

If only someone had bothered checking with the box office. A full hour before the doors opened, all 650 tickets for the show had been sold, and still the club was in a state of maddened siege.

Tony Nolan, of St. Albans, Vermont, was one of the throng of fans who wouldn't get into the Paradise that night. Two days before the show, he'd noticed an odd rattle in his old Escort's engine, and thought he'd better get it looked at before attempting to drive down to Boston. The mechanic took one look at the motor and told him he was lucky he'd even got across town; that wasn't an odd rattle he'd been hearing, it was a death rattle. Tony made the journey by Greyhound instead.

"I knew I was in trouble before we were even out of Vermont. It looked like everyone on the bus was going to the show, and most of them already had tickets. But I figured that if the worst came to the worst, I could get one off a scalper, and maybe I'd luck out and miracle one. I'd heard about that happening at Dead shows, how there was always someone with a ticket going spare, who'd let it go at face value or even less, and I knew that a lot of the people who followed Phish also followed the Dead. But I guess it just wasn't my night, and just to really rub it in, afterward I met up with some people I knew from Burlington, and they reckoned it was one of the best shows they'd ever seen."

They were probably right. From the moment they hit the stage, blazing into a stunning "I Didn't Know," Phish pulled out all the stops. No matter that they were essentially playing to a hometown audience, supplemented by a few curious locals and the club's bewildered staff; as the fans filed in, one of the bouncers asked if Phish was "a real band"; the question got back to the group, and they knew there was only one way to answer it.

Great swathes of *The Man Who Stepped into Yesterday* were included in the set, Led Zeppelin's "Good Times Bad Times," Jimi Hendrix's "Fire," and a greatest-hits selection from the last couple of years: "Golgi Apparatus," "Alumni Blues," "You Enjoy Myself," "Fee," "Fluffhead," and "Contact"—all leading up to that most stupendously unpredictable of workouts, "Big Black Furry Creature from Mars." And every roar of recognition from the capacity crowd sent another shock wave rippling through the Boston club scene. The best-kept secret in local rock lore was out. From here on in, Boston would be an open door for Phish.

Phish, however, had other matters on their mind. Demand for an official souvenir of their work, something more controlled than the live tapes which circulated so freely around their fan base, had been growing for over a year. Bootleg copies of *The Man Who Stepped into Yesterday* did make it out, but the band was understandably reluctant to sanction its release; the only viable alternative, then, was to present a new "debut" album.

Drawing from the Euphoria Sound demos of a year before, supplementing them with the results of a second set of sessions recorded in the weeks following the Paradise shows, and wrapping the tape in one of Jim Pollock's distinctive designs, *Junta* would be available on cassette only, at shows and by mail order. The album was titled, of course, in honor of Ben Hunter.

Aware that a lot was hanging on the album's success, not least of all the $5,000 they sank into recording it, Phish picked the contents carefully. *The Man Who Stepped into Yesterday* was overlooked completely; instead, they drew from a succession of what were already accepted Phish classics, turning in performances which could only emphasize that status. Certainly the version of "David Bowie" was the equal of any extant live recording, while the "Fluffhead" / "Fluff's Travels" suite expanded in a fashion which live improvisation never permitted, as the band themselves sorted through their own concert recordings, selecting the best ideas and the finest moments from so many old renderings and applying them all to what would, at least for the time being, remain the definitive rendering of this so-popular track.

"Fee" and "Dinner and a Movie," throwaway novelty songs in the shadow of the band's more deliberate epics, but essential components in the Phish arsenal nonetheless, were similarly stunning. Though the joyous inanity of the latter is arguably most effective live, when Phish's own antics can complement the lyrical lunacy, many fans still regard the studio take as the ultimate expression of the song's daft sentiments.

One of Phish's principle concerns, as *Junta* came together, was to establish their musical credentials in their own right, away from the morass of preconceptions which was flowering around them—flowering, and threatening to sweep them away.

The end of the 1980s was a strangely indecisive period in American rock 'n' roll tastes. Bands like the Pixies, Love and Rockets, the Replacements, and Jane's Addiction arose, seemingly out of nowhere, to snag the attention of an entire generation of listeners; leaving their early, independent roots behind them, inking pacts with the majors and MTV alike, this new wave of talent—"alternative bands," as a label-hungry media tagged them—was signposting the mood of the future, a hard, aggressive breed of pop music which wanted no truck with the conventions and moralities of old.

And it's true; a handful of these bands were making waves, although many more remained on the starting block in commercial terms, lauded by critics but ignored by the public. Depeche Mode and the Cure might have scored massive hits, but they were the exceptions, and by no means the rules.

In the marketplaces which really mattered, the old guard ruled: the Rolling Stones, with their once-every-half-decade stirring of the pot; the Who, reuniting one more time for a final farewell tour; Guns N' Roses, Los Angeles upstarts who lived a lifelong career in a matter of months, and were already into their dotage within three years of their debut; and of course, the Grateful Dead, an institution of such grizzled defiance that even the band members themselves probably forgot they'd never scored a hit single. Certainly everyone else had, which was why, when the Dead did suddenly vault into the Top Ten singles, with "Touch of Gray" in 1987, the shock waves shook the American music industry to its core. People had forgotten the group existed. No matter that the Dead toured almost nonstop for over twenty years, to the industry-at-large, they'd long since ceased to register, so self-contained did the band become.

It was as though they inhabited an alternate universe. Once in a while, when the Dead hit your town, the sheer enormity of their audience might impact on your consciousness, but only in a passing flash, a brief moment of wonderment—"Where do all these people come from?" Then you'd pass on, the crowds would thin out, and that would be it. You wouldn't think about them again until the next time they played.

"Touch of Gray" changed that forever. Suddenly Dead-heads were everywhere, and every age. A secret society was spewing from the earth, and no amount of ridicule could push it back down. Magazines which seemed to cater solely to the Dead suddenly began cropping up on Main Street news-stands, glossy psychedelic-looking things with names like *Relix, Dupree's Diamond News, Unbroken Chain*. They'd probably been around before, of course, but in the past they were always tucked way at the back, behind last month's *Rolling Stone* and the last remaining *Alternative Press*.

Newspapers began carrying Dead-related stories; all of a sudden, the police were on the band's fans' back, making massive busts aboard VW buses, then holding up a few ad-dled old hippies as proof that at last they were taking back the streets from the drug fiends and dropouts. No matter that smack, coke, and Ecstasy were taking a far greater toll on the American psyche than a few hits of acid were ever going to wreak, a bust is a bust, and the arrest figures soared.

A new language was evolving; sixties slang, which had lain moribund for years, was creeping back into everyday use. It was cool to be groovy, and far-out to be hip. Tie-dye shirts were back in fashion, for Christ's sake, and people were wear-ing patchouli oil again. It was only a matter of time before somebody latched on to a musical underground which could be applied to this same sudden comeback; it was only natural that whoever it was wouldn't have a clue what they were talk-ing about.

Blues Traveler were the first group to feel the heel of hindsight; like Phish, the band evolved on the East Coast, in Trey's own hometown of Princeton, New Jersey; like Phish, it was the vocalist and the drummer who got together first, when John Popper and Brendan Hill joined forces in 1983;

and like Phish, Blues Traveler's entire raison d'être was rooted in jam-packed improvisation.

And it was true that Blues Traveler made no secret of its allegiance to the Dead. John Popper was a familiar sight at Dead shows, gathering a crowd around him as he blew his omnipresent harp, and once his own band began picking up steam, he continued to sing the Dead's praises, and with good reason. They were discovered by David Graham, son of the legendary West Coast promoter Bill Graham; within months, Graham Senior was placing Blues Traveler onstage with Jerry Garcia, in the Dead's own San Francisco hometown.

But there the similarities ended. At that first show, Popper remembers being warned by Garcia's personal manager, "Okay, boys, no metal tonight," and, the singer continues, "I've always got the feeling that [the Dead] thought we were too . . . 'metal' is the word they use. But I think we're just younger."

In fact, the differences are far more profound. One early review of Blues Traveler described them as "an all-star tribute to the Moody Blues"; another remarked, "It's Hawkwind. Who become Metallica who become Genesis who become Richard Marx." Whether one approved of Blues Traveler's music or not, there was no denying their eclecticism, and their enrollment as charter members in the Sound-alike Dead Club was as superficial an observation as anything else which was written about Garcia's Grateful minstrels in the dawning days of their rebirth.

Other emergent groups, Widespread Panic, the Aquarium Rescue Unit, the Spin Doctors, and more, were tarred with similar brushes, and again, it was not for what they sounded like, but for the musical freedoms they espoused. They didn't sound like they'd just fallen off a computer nerd's hard drive, they weren't sallow-faced and spotty-chinned, whining songs about Generation X angst and agony, they weren't, in the parlance of the moment, "alternative." If only those tastemakers who condemned them with such disdain could have known precisely how mainstream "alternative" would have become, the entire history of the 1990s might have been very different.

For Phish, the growing rumblings about a distinct Dead-headedness to their music were even more obtrusive than for those other bands. Not only did such murmurings resurrect the age-old conflict between art and emotion which so colored Mike and Trey's early relationship, they also made a mockery of the incredible progress Phish had attained since it first got off the ground.

In the beginning the Dead were an influence. But so was Frank Zappa, so was Sun Ra, and maybe, if one of those had been magically reborn in the eyes of the media, Phish would now be fighting off comparisons with *My Brother the Wind* or *Weasels Ripped My Flesh*—neither of which, truth be told, they could have fought with such conviction.

The Dead, however, were long ago erased from the band's musical palette, and if Deadheads liked Phish, it was not because the two groups sounded the same. In fact, it was more likely to be because they didn't sound the same; after all, who needed an imitation, when the real thing was still going strong?

Both bands encouraged taping—but so did many others. Both bands enjoyed touring, and varied their sets to avoid stagnation; and both bands were sufficiently musically gifted not to be confined to any particular style. There was a common philosophy, then, and a similar disdain for those song-writing conventions which too often descended to clichés. But even there, the linkage was tenuous, rooted more around the recreational habits of a visible minority of Phish fans, and the unswerving devotion of a more anonymous mass, than any pronounced lifestyle decisions.

"For a long time," Fish mused, "the Dead were the only act out there that was taking any chances onstage." Now other groups were taking a similar step into the unknown, and "the crowd that was so concentrated on the Dead is saying, 'Hey, these guys are cool.'"

Mike told *Gallery of Sound Gazette*, "There's reasons to compare. There are similarities and there are differences. I personally really like the Dead a lot, so it doesn't offend me or anything." But he also acknowledged, "People that haven't heard us think that we are a Dead cover band or that we sound exactly like them. If they already have opinions about the Grateful Dead—like if they don't like the Dead, then they won't come to see us, whereas maybe they would like us anyway. That's one problem. Also, it just kind of gets old with clubs booking us as a Dead cover band. It's sort of a slap in the face when we are trying to do something unique."

Equally damaging, maybe even more so, were the inevitable drug links. The Dead's reputation as the ultimate musical acid trip, which of course was best experienced during an acid trip of one's own, had likewise fastened itself to Phish and their fans. The question was, would those fans—who spoke out so vehemently against musical stereotyping—fall headlong into that other cliché? "Our fans like to alter their consciousness," Mike mused. But he sincerely hoped that it was Phish's music, independent of the drug scene, which was the real consciousness-altering thing.

In print, or conversation, such arguments were convincing enough. But as they pieced together their first "real" album, Phish knew that conviction was only half of the battle. They also needed to produce an impeccable manifesto, of intent and imagination alike.

They succeeded, but only just. In their desperation to avoid certain comparisons, Phish inadvertently opened themselves up for others. Mike complained, "[Different people] said . . . one section of a song sounds like Zappa, one section of a song sounds like the Allman Brothers, and stuff like that"; and, listened to dispassionately, one can spot such elements: the medley of "Fluffhead" / "Fluff's Travels" boasts some particularly guilty, Zappa-esque segments.

But *Junta* was far more than a crazy patchwork of musical borrowings, as Mike affectionately reflects: "We really feel like there's something nice about that stage. In some ways, some people like it best. It has more of a youthful innocence in the way that the songs are patched together, different clumps sort of shoved together almost randomly. Like 'You Enjoy Myself' has twenty different sections, and there is a flow in the song, but it's not very maturely put together. A lot of the lyrics are, I think, the old-style lyrics for us where it's just wordplay, maybe with a couple of exceptions."

The only downside to *Junta*, in fact, was the speed with which it was rendered obsolete as Phish continued inducting new material into their set. By necessity alone, older songs, and that included much of the album, were already being shunted aside, a state of affairs which was only exacerbated that spring of 1989, when the band took on their first full-time lighting engineer.

SEXY NIGHTS, SEXY LIGHTS

Chris Kuroda may not have deliberately impacted upon Phish's musical dynamics, but the meshing of his own abilities with the band's desire to put on a genuinely spectacular show certainly saw their attention shift toward songs which would display both talents to their greatest extent.

Kuroda, a UVM student, first encountered Phish back in 1985. Looking to raise a little extra cash, Trey had recently commenced offering guitar lessons to other students, and in an online interview with writer Dean Budnick in 1995, Kuroda recalled, "I was in a band myself, and I wanted to get better, so I wanted to take lessons from Trey who . . . in my opinion, was the best guitar player going."

Kuroda had been studying for two or three weeks, when Trey asked him if he knew anybody who would be willing to help Phish carry their gear to and from shows, help them handle technical problems, and generally act as a trouble-shooter. The gig paid $20 a show. Kuroda laughs, "I said, 'Know someone? I'll do it, sure. So I started helping set stuff up, and carrying this and that."

He might have been doing that as well, had Chris Steck,

Phish's latest lighting engineer, not needed to visit the bathroom midway through a show at the Stone Church, Newmarket, on March 30, 1989.

Phish's lighting rig was not an impressive piece of technology, just eight tiny 300-watt bulbs, run from a correspondingly tiny board. But their standards were high, even if their wattage wasn't. Kuroda continued, "They'd had an ad in the paper for someone to do lights, and various people came in. [But] no one was very good at it, or no one could make the commitment." Chris Steck was just the latest in a long line of lighting men then, and according to Kuroda, Phish were already unhappy with him. At the Stone Church, however, something happened that changed their opinion completely. As the group came offstage, Trey made straight for Steck, to rave, "I finally really liked something that you did tonight and it was in 'Famous Mockingbird.' "

"And I thought to myself, 'Hmmm,' " smiles Kuroda. It was during "Famous Mockingbird" that Steck headed off to relieve himself. "So after, on the side, I went up to Trey and said, 'I just wanted you to know that he stepped out and I was doing that.' The following weekend there was another show, and Trey called me up that Thursday and said, 'The other guy's not going to be coming, so you're going to have to do it.' "

Kuroda was staggered. He'd never done lighting before; he'd never even thought about doing it before. But he hadn't been to what he calls "millions" of Dead shows, reveling in their own visual experience, without learning something. It would have blown him away if he'd known that within five years, the Dead themselves would approach him, asking him to work their lights, and that Candace Brightman, that band's regular designer, would be numbered among his biggest fans.

"The Dead offered me a job on three separate occasions. Not to be the designer, but to help out. As a kid I always thought, 'Wow, what a great thing that would be,' but I had to turn them down." He would also turn down an offer from the Electric Light Orchestra, arguing that he didn't feel experienced enough to operate their light show.

He was, of course, being modest. Making things up as he went along, learning for himself what worked and what didn't, Chris Kuroda has become one of the most accomplished lighting engineers on the American circuit; a long journey from the nervous hours he spent, in the spring of 1989, simply trying to figure out how best to illuminate the latest addition to Phish's live repertoire: twin trampolines, upon which Mike and Trey would bounce whilst continuing to play their instruments.

The spring of 1989 was a time of great import. Mike, Page, and Trey had all graduated from college and were throwing themselves into Phish full-time. Fish followed suit, taking a year off from Goddard (he would finally graduate in 1990, on the strength of a Senior Study titled *A Self-Teaching Guide to Drumming Written in Retrospect*), so that the band could rehearse and gig without interruption.

Phish were still widely regarded as a college draw at best, but it was plain, nevertheless, that they could make a living from their music, if only everybody shared the commitment. And no sooner was that decision made, than the final piece in the group's administrative jigsaw slipped effortlessly into place.

John Paluska, Phish's hardworking contact at Amherst College, also graduated that spring, moving straight from a classroom seat to the driver's seat; when Phish asked him to become their full-time manager, he showed no hesitation whatsoever. Dionysian Productions, the management company which Paluska and Junta Hunter designed exclusively to handle Phish, remains their primary point of contact with the business world around them, a self-sufficient and single-minded entity which has propelled Phish ever since.

Paluska bid farewell to Amherst with one final Phish show at the Zoo, on April 20, 1989. It was an eventful evening; just two songs into the set, during what was fast shaping up to be an epic rendering of "Fluffhead," the venue's fire alarms suddenly clanged into life. The hall was evacuated—thankfully, for a false alarm—and as the crowd filed back in, Phish were waiting to greet them with an impromptu version of the old Jeff Beck Group chestnut, "You Shook Me." A little later in the set, Phish reprised that unscheduled drama with a blazing rendering of Jimi Hendrix's "Fire."

Two months later, on June 9, Phish took their first bite out of the Big Apple, when they were booked into the Wetlands Preserve, a newly opened club on Hudson Street, in the deepest recesses of Tribeca, which *Rolling Stone* only vaguely slighted by describing as "an airy, hippie-ish downtown think tank."

Concessions stands, both inside the club and working from vans parked outside, offered a range of ecological souvenirs, everything from Save the Rainforests buttons to Grateful Dead posters on recycled paper. Over the entrance, the words "We Labor to Birth Our Dance with the Earth" welcomed the evening's revelers into the dark, wooded bar and stage area; watching the group set up, Larry Bloch, the club's proud owner, happily held court with anyone who wanted to approach him.

Wetlands was unique, even in a city teeming with uniqueness. According to Bloch, the club was "originally conceived of as a hangout place, not at all reminiscent of a concert hall, which is what many clubs are becoming these days. The vision included an intimate rapport, no video screens, but instead, lots of opportunity for direct experience, for taking the time to develop bands, for interaction among patrons and between the band and patrons, in short, for a total sharing of magic."

Everything about the Wetlands Preserve screamed anachronism, from the furnishings and decor, which defied the fashions of eighties nightclub chic, to an atmosphere which might have been carved wholesale from a Greenwich Village coffee bar in the early 1960s. Any moment, you expected to see the young Bob Dylan walk in, arm in arm with Joan Baez. "The big promoters want just a show," Bloch reasoned. "No vibe, no consciousness. I always thought rock 'n' roll meant treating the customer with respect, including fair ticket prices, at least two sets, letting in those under twenty-one even though they can't drink, things like this." Wetlands would swiftly become another staple of Phish's live itinerary.

And as Phish's range increased, so did their repertoire. New songs were appearing at the speed of light. "Reba," "Split Open and Melt," "Bathtub Gin," "The Mango Song," "My Sweet One," "Lawn Boy," "In a Hole," and the Gamehendge supplement "Punch Me in the Eye," all entered the band's set, while the group's arsenal of cover versions swelled by similar proportions. Gleefully, the quartet worked up unique renditions of the Everly Brothers' "Price of Love," the Guess Who's "Undone," Miles Davis's "All Blues," and Carole King's "You're No Good." Then they tried their hand at one that will eternally belie Phish's media image as a mere hippie jam band, at the same time it confirms their own comprehension of the intricacies of musical history.

The Sex Pistols' "Anarchy in the U.K." crashed into the group's set in October 1989, not as a statement of political nihilism, nor for the shock value which those opening, crashing chords were guaranteed to convey. They played it because, like so many of the other classics in Phish's litany, it's a great rock 'n' roll song.

On New Year's Eve, Phish confirmed their Boston ascendancy with a year's end show at the Exhibition Hall. They'd risen from Molly's to the World Trade Center in just twelve months, but even Phish could never have known that they would return to ever-grander Boston stages every New Year's for the next half-decade.

In keeping with the pre-gig publicity's stated desire for "creative formal attire," Trey, Page, and Mike opened the show in tuxedos and tails, singing Fish's vacuum-cleaner showstopper, "I Didn't Know."

Fish himself, though, was nowhere in sight. The verses went on, and the crowd, expecting the drummer to have something up his sleeve, braced itself for what would inevitably come next. In fact, there was nothing whatsoever up his sleeve, for the simple reason that he didn't have any sleeves. He emerged onstage naked but for a top hat and g-string. How could Phish top that? How could the new year, even the new decade, top that?

Well, it could start by introducing Phish to some of the other bands who were sharing their journey into the heart of the jam.

In February 1990, Phish shared the stage with Widespread Panic for the first time, doing a brace of shows in Georgia which the local-boys-making-good would headline, and a handful in the Northeast, with roles reversed, in front of the Phish faithful.

With their *Space Wrangler* album already gaining plaudits on the underground circuit, and their own improvisational skills the talk of the scene, Widespread Panic, like Blues Traveler, evinced an in-concert musical purity and spontaneity which made them ideal bedmates for Phish. Having felt themselves to be out in the musical cold for so long, so totally divorced from whichever musical upheavals were convulsing the music scene that week, it was suddenly amazing how Phish were now encountering genuine contemporaries everywhere they turned.

Not every band with whom Phish worked was so welcoming, of course. Shawn Brice, of the highly rated electronic band Battery, recalls, "it was the spring of 1990, at Bennington College in Vermont. Battery was performing at a festival along with many other bands. Some of the known talent were Blues Traveler, Spin Doctors, Lunachicks, 24-7 Spies.

"While we were playing, some guy dropped the contents of his bottle of Rolling Rock onto the mixing board. This caused one of the channels to go out. Since our music is entirely electronic, we basically lost all sound. We had to take a break, and start over. After the problems seemed to be fixed, we started again. Then it happened again! The sound was horrible, but we continued playing.

"At this point, the lead singer of Phish walked by, and threw his cigarette at me. It hit me just above my left eyebrow. I decided to be professional about this, and ignored him. A few seconds later I saw smoke coming from my keyboard (a DX-7; it happened to be my very first keyboard). I looked down to see the control panel beginning to melt. For some strange reason, I stifled the urge to jump around my keyboard and kill the fucker."

Elsewhere, however, Phish's hijinx won them nothing but admiration.

The immortally named Aquarium Rescue Unit, with whom Phish shared a D.C. bill in June of that year, was another outfit with whom Phish would forge an instant camaraderie. An Atlanta-based group which Trey once described, lovingly of course, but also mysteriously, as "the sickest group of musicians onstage at any one time," the Aquarium Rescue Unit was led at that time by Colonel Bruce Hampton, himself one of the true Hall-of-Famers on the American music scene.

The Colonel jokes that he's been making music longer than most of his bandmates and fans have been living (he started in 1963). His first album, recorded with the Hampton Grease Band back in 1969, is proudly ranked the worst-selling double album in Columbia Records' history. According to legend, label head Clive Davis hated it so much that he stopped the presses after just 30,000 copies.

Hampton remains unrepentant. The Aquarium Rescue Unit, he reckons, "has continued with some of the ideas I had back in the sixties with the Grease Band," a furious amalgam of avant-garde blues and psychedelic jazz. "Only now, I think people have been exposed to enough different kinds of music that they can grasp what we're doing." Back in 1969, people didn't know what to make of it, and to prove his point, the Aquarium Rescue Unit's 1992 live album was filled with old Grease Band numbers.

Like Widespread Panic, the Aquarium Rescue Unit would become one of the first signings to Phil Walden's newly reactivated Capricorn label, following in the equally distinctive, but one-generation-removed footsteps of the Allman Brothers and the Marshall Tucker Band. "We plug in and play from the heart," Hampton once boasted. "We don't ever rehearse, because rehearsing tends to take the spontaneity out of a performance and make everything too predictable. It's more fun when things take a new twist every time you step onstage."

Talking to *Relix*, Widespread Panic vocalist John Bell detailed a similar modus operandi. "It's always been a live situation for us. Our music is honest. It's made for the sake of being in a band, and it just comes out naturally. A lot of people like to be surprised, and wherever we play, it seems we're either right on the verge, or smack in the middle of something new. And if it's new to us, it's got to be a surprise for others. Music should be exciting for everybody all at once.

It's also about an evolving process, rather than a grand design."

Nowhere was the importance, and value, of this evolution better documented than in the habits of the bands' most devoted fans. Loyal to the point of obsession, the crowds whom the media was just beginning to tag, with a deafening lack of originality, Phish Heads and Spread Heads, thought nothing of trekking miles to see their heroes—the turnout at Phish's Paradise gig was simply the tip of a traveling iceberg. Every time the group touched down, there would be a crop of familiar faces waiting, a crop which increased, it seemed, with every passing month.

"We have a certain percentage of fans who have left mainstream society for a while, to go on tour with us," Mike told *Bass Player* magazine. "For them, our music is just the theme of their lives, the background music."

It was not only fans who traveled, either. Individual band members have lost count of the number of times they have fallen into conversation with a total stranger, only to find that the earnest face and encouraging smile conceals a snakepit full of arcane musical knowledge, drawn from a library of live tapes which would take a lifetime to listen through completely.

Obscure snippets of music dropped into a song at a half-forgotten gig would suddenly be presented for dissection, and the demands for explanations left the musicians reeling. Yet they tried to answer anyway, scouring their minds for a hint of a memory, because they understood how important such things were to people. Now they understood why.

Phish themselves had only recently begun taping their own shows, but as Paul Languedoc can testify, fans were documenting the band's growth for as long as he'd been on board; even longer, if some of the conversations he'd enjoyed with various tapers were anything to go by.

It was, everybody reasoned, another side effect of the audience's affinity with the Deadhead community, like the tie-dye shirts, the patchouli and Volkswagen buses which already followed Phish around. After a very hesitant, and sometimes hostile, start, the Dead had ultimately encouraged fans to tape their concert. And for years, they did. Not surprisingly, a vast network of traders developed, and a sprawling mass of reference, eventually compiled into the multivolume Deadbase encyclopedia, built up around them. By the time the Dead themselves set about documenting their live career for their own archives, there were already fans out there who'd been doing the same thing for years.

It was not the depth of these archives that was most impressive, however. It was the fact that the activities of the tapers were having a very pronounced, and very beneficial, effect upon the band itself. For Phish, this realization, vague though it had been for several years now, finally hit home hard in April 1990.

Phish were booked into another series of shows in Colorado, and, Mike marvels, "People had already heard of us because of tapes. Word of mouth . . . spread through tapes." From here on in, the band's once casual attitude toward tapers solidified to the extent that when Phish finally began talking with major record companies, one of their strongest stipulations was that taping could continue unmolested.

Today, Phish themselves maintain an archive which strives to preserve every available recording of the band in concert, and like the Dead's own, better-known tape vault, this priceless resource only exists because of the efforts and obsessions of Phish's fans. The group's decision, in 1993, to open up a "taper's section" at every show they played was very much their way of thanking the countless collectors who were out there with their Walkmans a decade ago, docu-

menting concerts even Phish did not think were worth pre-
serving.

The spring 1990 Colorado tour included shows in Boulder, Crested Butte, Denver, and Colorado Springs, a string of
dates which Phish viewed both as an opportunity to spread
the word and a chance to debut some more new material,
away from the analytical eyes of their home crowd.

The monstrous jam vehicle "Tweezer," "Cavern," "Uncle
Pen," and "Runaway Jim" were all introduced into the set on
this outing, while the Colorado crowd, which of course included a number of people who'd first caught Phish in Telluride the year before, wasn't alone in receiving some
memorable dates. One night, Trey told the audience that
Chris Kuroda was looking for a date for the night, while Fish
gleefully chanted, "Sexy lights, sexy lights."

"I got the date," Kuroda laughs. "She was actually a
friend, but she chose that opportunity to get to know me
better.

Marty Cane, a student at Colorado College in Colorado
Springs, was one of several who went to Phish's first performance in that city, "more because it was something to do that
night than anything else."

Though it lies little more than an hour from Denver, Colorado Springs was a very rare stop on any touring band's
itinerary in the early 1990s, the victim of both a hard-hitting
local recession and the city's reputation for being split equally
between right-wing religious groups and even-farther-right–
wing military factions—it is topped and tailed by the U.S. Air
Force Academy and a major army base, with the underground
headquarters of NORAD (North American Air Defense
Command) not too far away, either. When Donny Osmond's
Soldier of Love (what else?) tour is the biggest thing to hit
town all year, you know you're in trouble. Either that or a
black hole.

"A few kids had heard of Phish, and there were some people who came in from out of town," Marty continues, "but no one I knew had much idea of what they were all about. By the time the show was over, though, I don't think there was anyone in the room who wasn't completely converted. I remember afterward, we virtually forced the band to promise they'd be back soon." Phish returned to Colorado Springs for Halloween.

Colorado also saw Phish begin to seriously revise the material they were recording for their second album.

Lawn Boy was taped throughout 1989, with the first sessions, at Archer Studios in Winooski, Vermont, kicking off within days of *Junta*'s May release. And whereas their debut album saw Phish working to preserve their vast live set in the studio, *Lawn Boy* was intended to evidence their mercurial growth with the introduction of newer material, which they deliberately refrained from performing in concert. Instead, they wanted to let the live versions grow from the studio's seeds. Mike put it best: "The songs were formed in the studio, so they could fall into an album."

The luxury of so much studio time was hard-won, of course. The previous fall, Phish entered and won Boston's annual Rock 'n' Roll Rumble, competing against some of the city's best unsigned bands. The studio time was their prize.

Trey continues, "Our . . . philosophy for this album was that we weren't going to play any of the stuff live until after we'd done the album, which is what most people do anyway." That way, once the songs were introduced to the concert stage, fans would compare them to their studio incarnations and not, as is often, damagingly, the case, the other way around.

It was a smart move. "The Squirming Coil," *Lawn Boy*'s opening number, had never been performed live before it was

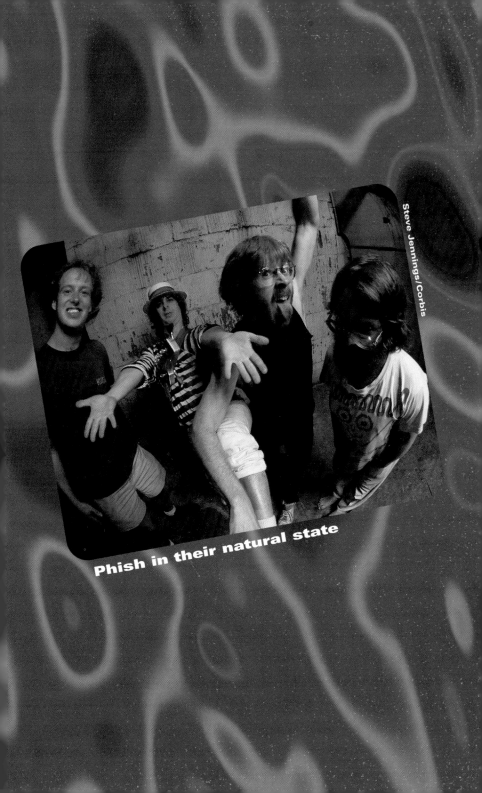

Steve Jennings/Corbis

Phish in their natural state

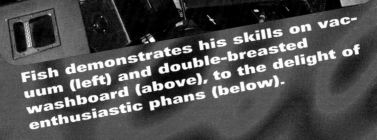

Fish demonstrates his skills on vacuum (left) and double-breasted
washboard (above), to the delight of
enthusiastic phans (below).

Ye Olde Clifford Ball

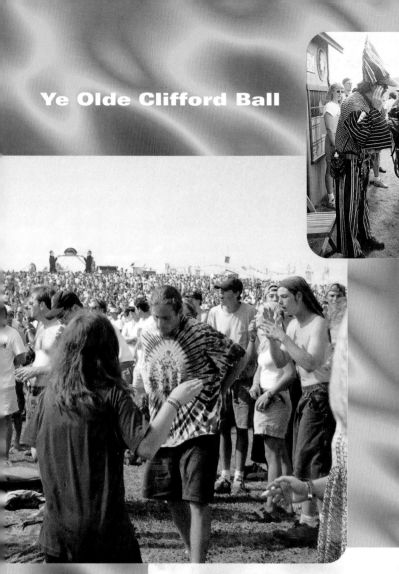

Page McConnell

Trey Anastasio

Mike Gordon

Jon Fishman

A Phish post-pheeding phrenzy

recorded, yet it quickly came to rank among Phish's most popular numbers. Indeed, many fans continue to regard it as the quintessential Phish song; certainly it was one which Trey would single out in a *Rolling Stone* interview in 1992:

"We've found that people who come to see us live are really listening," he remarked. "They understand our music. They get it. People write us letters like, 'I really like the fact that "The Squirming Coil" modulates.' People notice that." Then, as though consciously recoiling from Fish's stated belief that Phish are "the nerd band of rock 'n' roll" he added, "But not most people, of course."

Not all the songs were new, of course. "Run Like an Antelope," "Reba," "My Sweet One," and the delicious, horn-powered "Split Open and Melt" were stage veterans, while the album closed with "Oh Kee Pah Ceremony," a song which had been in the set since 1987, and a reprise of "Fee," lifted straight from the now-deleted *Junta* for fans who missed out last time around.

Lawn Boy was scheduled for release early in 1990, on the independent Absolute A-Go-Go label, a small company with big affiliations. The label was distributed nationwide through the renowned Rough Trade network, guaranteeing that *Lawn Boy* would infiltrate every record shop around, from the mightiest chain-store conglomerates to the tiniest mom-and-pop outlets.

A total of 10,000 copies of *Lawn Boy* were manufactured, and with Rough Trade swinging behind it, *Lawn Boy* was close to selling out within months of its release. Phish themselves simply couldn't carry enough copies with them when they went on the road, but every night, their mailing list would gather up another couple hundred names and addresses.

And then the whole thing came tumbling down. Overnight, and within weeks of *Lawn Boy*'s appearance in the stores, the British-based distribution company collapsed, a victim not only of the latest recession to rush through the American music industry, but also of the growing weight of competition from the "major" labels.

When Rough Trade first started in the heyday of punk rock, it was little more than a record store in west London, which invited new artists to consign their self-produced singles for sale in the store. Five years later, when Rough Trade first moved into the American market, it continued working on those same rudimentary principles. Concentrating upon acts which a larger company would never have even looked at, and financing itself with the handful of acts who did go on to greater things (the Smiths were a Rough Trade discovery), the company was perhaps the grassroots success story of the 1980s, respected for its principles, regaled for its taste.

But Rough Trade's death did more than spell the end for a kind of idealism which flew in the face of industry capitalism. It also crushed the myriad groups and labels whose product Rough Trade distributed, but who could now do nothing more than join a long line of creditors. Phish could not even retrieve their master tapes from the wreckage of the company.

Reeling from such an enormous blow, Phish immediately set themselves to clawing their way back. Announcing that they were going to take three months off the road, their first substantial break in five years, the band scheduled themselves into Wendell Studios in New York, tentatively planning to begin work on a successor to the ill-fated *Lawn Boy*.

Beyond an obvious need to replace the album on store shelves as quickly as possible, there were several other reasons Phish were so keen to get back to work. Both musically and conceptually, *Lawn Boy* was already outgrown—they had, after all, recorded it almost twelve months before. Trey was also thinking seriously about the Gamehendge saga once more. The success of individual songs from the cycle had long since cemented the concept in the hearts of Phish's audience, and two of these songs, "Possum" and the thematic "The Man Who Stepped into Yesterday," were to be recorded during the band's Wendell sojourn.

"Tweezer," "Harry Hood," "Runaway Jim," and a newly arranged, slow version of "Rift" were also recorded, but the end results were less than brilliant. Although a bootleg tape of the session did make it into circulation, Phish scrapped the recording in its entirety. Despite the commercial success of their studio recordings, the group's forte remained its live performance, and that was what they now decided to concentrate upon. At least for the time being.

The remainder of the summer was spent furiously writing and rehearsing new material, and on September 13, Phish re-emerged from hibernation with an astonishing Wetlands gig; astonishing, because almost 50 percent of the set comprised new material: the fugue "The Asse Festival," "Buried Alive," Page's "Magilla," "Stash," and "Tube," were all premiered at that show, together with covers of the Doobie Brothers' "Minute by Minute," Earl Scruggs's "Paul and Silas," and Champion Jack Dupree's "Going Down Slow," which Trey first heard on Duane Allman's posthumous *Anthology* collection.

There was also an onstage reappearance for Steve Pollack, in his Dude of Life character. His irregular guest spots with the group were always divisive; for all those fans who consider him an integral part of the Phish philosophy, there are as many who regard him as an unnecessary diversion at best, an absurd irritation at worst.

Certainly the Wetlands crowd was restive, even as Phish accompanied him through three brand-new songs ("Dahlia," "I Don't Care About Anybody But Myself," and "Revolution's Over"), and over the next year, the Dude's appearances would become increasingly controversial.

Undeterred, the Dude and Phish would maintain a close relationship, culminating with a series of studio dates in early 1991, at which time a full Dude of Life album was recorded, chiefly comprising songs which Phish themselves were regularly playing at this time. And still, when Phish reached Tuscaloosa the following November, great swaths of the audience actually walked out of the room until his segment was complete.

On October 6, 1990, Phish opened for Blues Traveler at the Capitol Theatre in Portchester, New York. The evening's venue was a significant choice for two bands whose stock-in-trade is the proliferation of dreams; nineteen years before, the theater was the setting for one of the most unusual experiments ever performed at a rock concert, when the Grateful Dead hooked into a dream telepathy experiment being run at the Maimonides Dream Laboratory in Brooklyn.

Every night, the audience would be shown an art print, and while the Dead played on, the crowd would be asked to try and project the image to a sleeper forty-five miles away. Four nights out of the six, the watching scientists reported direct hits. Phish's show at that same venue may not have bragged so scientific an impact, but still, their fans maintain, it was the kind of show that dreams are made from . . . which was just as well, as the following night's gig possessed all the makings of a genuine nightmare.

Five minutes before showtime, Club Bene in Sayerville, New Jersey, was virtually empty, maybe fifty people sitting around waiting. Peeping around the massive curtain which hung over the stage, Trey recognized a handful of faces, a few from Boston, a few from New York, one guy he remembered from the Clark University shows. The group decided to start the show with something a little different. Trey remembers, "We had the curtain coming up and did the *My Three Sons* foot thing." Then, rewarding the tiny crowd for even bothering to turn out, Phish launched into a colossal performance which reached as far afield as Gamehendge and old ZZ Top.

Tactics like this worked, as well, on the occasions when Phish would convert a near-empty venue into a de facto rehearsal room, then turn in a show which veered deliriously between wild experimentation and deliberate corniness, anything to keep the audience involved. A mere dozen people might have understood what was happening, but they'd tell their friends, and their friends would spread the word a bit further, and the next time Phish played, the whole club might be full of people eager to see these four crazy guys from Vermont. And clubs full of people eventually start attracting attention.

"Way back in early 1990," *Pollstar* magazine recalled a few years later, "clubs began reporting concert grosses from a band called Phish. Month after month they came in, dozens of grosses, virtually all of them sold-out shows."

Pollstar is the industry's largest guide to what really goes on when a band is on tour, a library of attendance figures and concert grosses, and the only place to look if you need to know how well so-and-so's latest tour *really* did. And it was baffled.

A check of the enormous database which the company maintains revealed that Phish hadn't even registered before the 1989 New Year's show; the six years the band spent on the road before then, slogging around college campuses, bars, and cafes, might as well not have happened. Only when a group reaches a certain level does it register on Artist Tour History reports. But rarely did any "unknown" outfit register this strongly.

Back in February, Phish played the Living Room in Providence, Rhode Island: 620 tickets, sold out. The Boston Paradise: 650, sold out. Wetlands in March: 600, sold out. The Boulder Theater in April: 930, sold out. The Bayou in D.C.: 500, sold out; and so on through the year.

By Christmas, as *Pollstar* began tabulating the year's most successful concert acts, Phish registered twenty-one shows on the concert hotwire, and filled nineteen of them. A total of 15,536 people had seen them play, spending $147,072 for the privilege. And that wasn't counting all the shows which passed unreported: If one simply counts up the number of different live tapes which exist, Phish played close to 100 shows in 1990. Add in all the gigs which weren't recorded, and that figure more than doubles.

Yet somehow, they completely slipped under the radar. "Phish had a manager in Massachusetts no one had ever heard of, and that was it," *Pollstar* marveled. "No record label, no booking agency, nothing."

A lot of the people reading *Pollstar*'s early accounts, contemplating this minor miracle occurring in the Northeast, laughed out loud and checked the calendar. A belated April Fool's, right? Things like that didn't happen anymore, not with a hundred record labels out there, all scratching around for the next big thing, and signing anything that moved if they thought it could sell. Bands simply didn't explode out of nowhere like that, then carry on exploding. And they certainly didn't do it in New York, Boston, and places like that. If *Pollstar* wasn't pulling its readership's chain, then someone else was pulling *Pollstar*'s.

It was only when, or if, those doubters dug deeper, that they realized what was really going on.

On December 28, 1990, Sue Drew, an A&R staffer at Elektra Records in New York, entered the New York Marquee, as one later chronicler put it, "expecting to hear a band." Instead, she discovered an entire culture. "The scene at the Marquee is late 1960s," *Life* magazine marveled. "Long, untended hair, baggy, tie-dyed clothes, a friendly sense of community bolstered by booze and grass." It was like a slice of Haight-Ashbury in the heart of New York City; it was, to reiterate Charles Hirschberg's incredulous report, like something out of the late 1960s . . . in the early 1990s.

Drew was alerted to Phish by the grapevine; not the word on the streets, though, but the word in the boardrooms, the scratching of heads which echoed through the mahogany halls as some very powerful music-industry people began to realize that something was going on—and they didn't have a clue what it was.

If *Pollstar* was to be believed, Phish were a phenomenon out of nowhere, and that's what attracted Sue Drew. That is also what encouraged the highest echelons of Elektra to back her as strongly as they did. They'd checked the grosses and asked around at the clubs. Within five years, company chairman Bob Krasnow proudly predicted, Phish would be selling platinum. "Metallica, Mötley Crüe, 10,000 Maniacs, weren't selling a lot of records when we signed them, and they are all tour-driven bands. I think Phish will have a double-platinum record in a year or two."

Back at the Marquee, Sue Drew was about to experience just what it was that got Krasnow so excited. "The lights dim," Charles Hirschberg wrote, "and the sounds that explode from the stage are outrageous. The audience twirls and whirls ecstatically in a kind of free-form ballet called noodle dancing. The kids are rapt, responding to the music with an intensity Drew has never seen before."

Phish's set that night was typical—typical, that is, for a group for whom nothing but the bizarre is customary. Opening their first set with "Runaway Jim," opening the second with "The Landlady," and treating the sold-out audience to one of the deadliest takes on "Tweezer" on record, Phish wrapped up the evening with "Bouncing Around the Room" and "Highway to Hell."

John Popper turned up to add some impassioned harmonica to the end of the set, and the growing battalion of tapers exchanged gleeful looks. Blues Traveler fans were always willing to trade well for recordings featuring their hero. Drew, feeling more and more like a gate-crasher at a secret society, slipped out without a word. There was a lot of thinking for her to do.

But she was back a few nights later, her mind made up. If it was the last thing she did, she determined, Phish would become Elektra recording artists. And Phish could not have been more underwhelmed by any of it.

Twenty-two years before, under almost identical circumstances, another Elektra A&R man, Danny Fields, wandered backstage at another unsigned, unknown band's gig, introduced himself and expected their gratitude. Instead, he got Iggy Pop and the Stooges.

Drew made the same introductions. She received indifference. "They could not have cared less," she admitted later. As far as Phish were concerned, they were already doing what they wanted to do. Having a "real" record label working behind them would simply throw new ballplayers into the game, and Phish really didn't know if they needed them. They took Drew's card, agreed that someone would call her, and got on with packing their gear up. John Paluska would follow through on that promise sometime in the new year. Phish, in the meantime, had another gig the next night to prepare for.

"Let's say we play until two," Trey once outlined. "We get to the hotel by four. We sleep exactly eight hours, and get woken by the maids at noon. We hobble out to the van. We try to find a Denny's. We eat breakfast, drive for four hours, get out of the van just in time for a sound check. We sit backstage for two hours eating some kind of measly meal. Then we go onstage, play until two, get to the hotel by four. . . ." And it all went round again.

New England remained the stronghold to which Phish would never tire of returning, but they were reaching deeper and deeper into the country too. In February 1991, a solid stretch of shows took Phish from the New York Marquee through D.C., and on to such exotic locales as Richmond, Virginia, and Charlottesville, North Carolina; the student stronghold of nearby Chapel Hill, and down to Knoxville, Tennessee; through the musical meccas of Nashville, Memphis, and Atlanta; deep into Alabama and Louisiana.

Up to the friendly heights of Colorado, through the skiing resorts of Breckenridge and Aspen; on to a couple of nights in the sauna that is Steamboat, Colorado's famed—and aptly named—Inferno. By the end of March, Phish were in California, for shows at the DNA Lounge in San Francisco, Berkeley Square, Berkeley, and the International Beer Garden in Arcata.

The Pacific Northwest was next, and then it was into the home stretch : Wisconsin, Illinois, Michigan, Ohio, and back to Vermont by the end of April . . . just in time to head out again for the summer and fall tours. Phish would not be stationary for a moment; it was as if, by staying in the ballroom, they could forget what was going on in the boardroom. John Paluska had made that call to Elektra, now they were talking every day. And a deal, as they say, was imminent. There were just a few more things to iron out.

On July 13, the audience at the Berkshire Performing Arts Center in Lenox, Massachusetts, was treated to the onstage debut of the Giant Country Horns, an ensemble whose tireless hooting and tooting brought whole new dimensions to Phish's repertoire. All three Horns were old friends; tenor saxophonist Russ Remington worked with Phish back in the days of the Johnny B. Fishman Jazz Ensemble; alto player Dave Grippo and trumpeter Carl Gerhard completed the lineup. They got into the spirit of things as well, leaping aboard their own miniature trampolines and bouncing away with the best of them. But a few fans weren't happy with this latest development, and as the summer tour plowed on, the reasons for their fears grew apparent.

Phish spent a month working out horn charts with the trio, leading them through a bewildering repertoire of songs, old and new. But short of teaching the Giant Country Horns every song they knew, the band were by necessity restricted to a considerably abridged catalog—and of all Phish's best-loved idiosyncracies, their refusal to play the same set twice is one of the most legendary.

They managed to vary the set considerably, of course, working up close to seventy different songs, including a couple of unique covers (Charlie Parker's "Moose the Mooche," Fish's solo spotlight rendering of the Doors' "Touch Me"), but there were no new songs, no real surprises, and as one fan noted a few years later in the *Pharmer's Almanac*, the Horns' absence from the August 3 show at Amy Skelton's Larabee Farm in Auburn, Maine, came as a welcome relief "to all those who had grown tired of similar set lists during the July tour."

The Larabee Farm show was one of the most eagerly awaited events of the summer. A month before, Phish joined the bill for the two-day Arrowhead Ranch festival in Parksville, New York, sharing the stage with the Spin Doctors, the Authority, TR3, and the Radiators. Unlike those other outfits, though, Phish would play both days, with the second one ranking among the very best of the entire Giant Country Horns–fired tour.

It was after that second show that Trey announced the Larabee Farm gig, a free festival for everyone who had followed Phish so far, and even the band was amazed at the dedication that the announcement inspired.

The Horns notwithstanding, everyone, it seemed, was at Larabee: the Dude of Life, who wandered on and off the stage seemingly at will; Sophie Dilloff, the future Mrs. Page McConnell, who joined the Dude for a rendition of "She's Bitchin' Again"; and in the audience, pretty much anyone you'd ever seen at a Phish gig. One fan traveled over 3,000 miles to be there, a feat which Phish themselves duly recognized a month later in Buffalo, when they dedicated the entire show to him.

The Buffalo gig, of course, was part of Phish's next tour, their third of the year and the most arduous they'd ever undertaken. It lasted nine weeks, an exhausting routine which returned them to every corner of the country, and a few more stops in between. "We covered a bit more ground in less time than we had before, so there was a lot of driving," Mike sighed. "But it was very well organized, geographically and stuff."

Unlike the summer tour, the fall outing saw Phish breaking in a number of new songs. "It's Ice," "Sparkle," "Brother," and "Glide" all proved how Phish spent the brief month since the Larabee Farm show. But it was the jazzy "All Things Reconsidered," an improvisation based around the theme to National Public Radio's *All Things Considered*, rolled out as an encore in New Hampshire on September 25, which was the biggest hit. The song instantly proved itself the perfect vehicle for Phish's most imaginative instincts; in fact, it almost proved itself too perfect. "All Things Reconsidered" was simply so technical that it would take another nine months of revision before the band were ready to tackle it again.

"It's a perfect example of theme and variation," Trey explained a couple of years later. "The art of songwriting is coming up with catchy ideas, and the art of composition is taking those catchy ideas and developing them without bringing in new material. It's a really good exercise because it teaches you how to improvise on an established theme. For us, it's good discipline, since we can lock together like a jigsaw puzzle to reach the same point musically two minutes later, a place we never could have gotten to if we were just playing spontaneously."

Again, the shows were a virtual free-for-all for the Phish family. Fish's mother, Mimi, and the Dude of Life reprised their roles as honorary Phish, and Colonel Bruce Hampton and the Aquarium Rescue Unit, opening the show in New Orleans, proved that they could jam with the best of them by joining Phish for a truly inspired "David Bowie." Every night, it seemed, boasted its special moment, a special memory.

But it was within the distinctly uninspiring surroundings of the North Shore Surf Club in Olympia, Washington, that Phish pulled out the biggest surprise, when they launched into what was only the second-ever complete performance of Gamehendge. Just one song, "Lizards," slipped out of the set, and critics have pointed out that Trey's narration did not always follow the specific sequence of the original production. Such concerns are little more than nitpicking, however. It was three years since Phish last visited Gamehendge; it might be three more before they returned there. For the five hundred lucky souls who packed the club not knowing what to expect, history had been made.

It would continue to be made four nights later, as well. On October 17, Phish became the first unsigned group from Vermont, or anywhere else for that matter, to sell out San Francisco's Great American Music Hall—two nights running.

Their timing could not have been better. In little more than a month, they would be an unsigned group no longer.

Like Phish, John Paluska spent a lot of time wondering precisely what Elektra could offer. And what it was they wanted.

It is, of course, the nature of the music industry to want in on every party in town, and if anything surprised him, it was that it took so long for Phish to actually get noticed. Without drawing unwanted comparisons, Blues Traveler were picked up over a year before, signing to A&M amid a wave of industry interest, and Phish's draw was certainly on a par with theirs.

There again, Blues Traveler also had the full weight of the Bill Graham organization behind them. Phish matched that with a couple of guys working out of an office on Harvard Street, in Waltham, Massachusetts. Blues Traveler opened gigs for Lynyrd Skynyrd and Jerry Garcia. Phish opened gigs for Blues Traveler. And Blues Traveler enjoyed some very aggressive marketing. In comparative terms, Phish didn't even know what marketing was. Once Paluska had thought about it some more, maybe Phish's continued obscurity wasn't so surprising.

As Paluska's negotiations with Elektra began, the question was, Did they want to leave that obscurity behind? Did they even need to? And what would be the cost if they decided that they did?

PEOPLE TALK ABOUT SEX A LOT

Shell McLennan recorded her first Phish concert in April 1991, at the Starry Night in Portland, Oregon. She'd never heard the band before; she wasn't even sure she'd heard of them. But a friend called her up, bought her a ticket, and loaned her his Walkman. He couldn't make the show, so would she go instead?

At first she said no. She'd been to enough shows to know that even if the headliners were cool about taping, you still needed to negotiate the bouncers and security, and all the other hired hands who didn't give a shit what the band told people. There's a sign on the door that says, No Cameras, No Tape Recorders, and that sign is the law.

Phish, she was assured, would be different, and as it turned out, they were. No heavy hands patting her down at the door, no beady eyes watching while she unwrapped her C90, just an odd-looking guy with an anorak and glasses, and a tape deck the size of mission control, who sneered at her gear as he adjusted his mikes.

"I guess you won't be wanting a patch," he sniffed, and Shell didn't have a clue what he meant. From the stench of grass which hung over the room, he was probably trying to sell her some drugs. She moved away, stood fairly stage-center, pressed down a button and let the tape do the rest. Phish were halfway through their second set before she realized she'd forgotten to turn the tape over. She'd been so carried away by the music.

Five years later, she can still recall the thrill of that night, because she can still experience it. Her tape was a washout, but the bespectacled anorak came over later, and when she told him what had happened, he took down her address. Two days later, he'd mailed her a tape, near-perfect fidelity, and such perfect stereo, it could have come off a CD.

But that wasn't the point. The point was, without the bespectacled anorak, and people like him, the music Phish made every night would have been lost forever, would have soared out into deepest space someplace, or wherever it is that sounds go once you've heard them. Forget the laws about bootlegging, that was what the real crime was.

That was also one of the biggest sticking points in Phish's ongoing negotiations with Elektra—the band's unreserved support for taping. "If we have a great experience playing," Mike reasoned, "why not let people have a souvenir of it? Even if it's not the same experience listening to the tape, it's something."

Since the Colorado tour first showed them how a network of fans can spring up simply through exchanging cassette tapes of concerts, Phish went even farther out of their way to encourage fans to record shows, and not only because it helped spread the word.

"In a little way, it encourages us to be spontaneous," Mike once raved. "If people are taping us every night, we're not going to be playing the same show."

These arguments met blank stares at Elektra. In the suited

halls of record-company power systems, live taping means only one thing—bootlegging, that so-called bane of the industry toward whose destruction untold man-hours and money have been directed, all to no avail.

Phish refused to budge, and five years later, Mike would admit, "Elektra has been a great record company. They understand that we're a phenomenon. We were before we signed with the record label, so they let us do what we want. Taping's a big issue . . . but they let us do it, and it's questionable whether it affects our record sales." In fact, it's questionable whether it affects anyone's sales. Even the music industry's own sources admit that bootleg recordings actually consume a minute portion of the money spent on music every year—published estimates vary between one and three percent. What they do do, on the other hand, is ensure that a rising talent continues rising (Phish, of course, were bootlegged long before they got a record deal); that a struggling group at least retains its visibility (Big Country, and Love and Rockets, were both bootlegged after they were dropped); and that a collectible band remains collectible.

"Record companies bleat on about bootlegs stealing money from the music industry, and ripping the kids off," one New York dealer told *Alternative Press* magazine in 1996. "But whenever [a major band's new] album is released, it outsells their bootlegs by ten to one in my store. The only people who bought the boots were people who'd already bought all the official releases, who'd bought the CD singles for the bonus tracks, and probably bought all the T-shirts as well. They're not dupes, or thieves or anything else. They're just fans, who like the band and want to hear more. And if the record companies won't give it to them, then someone else will. It's called supply and demand." And Phish knew that no matter how much new music they supplied, they could never meet the demand for more. Once Elektra conceded that point, the remainder of the deal would be reasonably plain sailing.

Although several other labels, once they got wind of Elektra's interest, did make a pitch for Phish, the company's offer remained the only one which the band seriously considered. The label's size had much to do with that. Although Elektra has, over the years, bragged the kind of artist roster which could fill a sizable record collection, it had stubbornly remained a small, and select, company.

In its earliest dealings with rock 'n' roll in the late 1960s, eclectic talents like the Doors, the MC5, the Stooges, and the Incredible String Band could never have survived without Elektra taking a chance on their eclectic charms, while the label's early-to-mid-seventies heyday saw it playing a major part in the West Coast singer/songwriter scene, long before the likes of Joni Mitchell and David Ackles became a part of the mainstream.

Elektra took chances. In 1973, when every other label in America reacted with laughter, the company had signed Jobriath, America's first glam-rock supernova, and even today, an attributed influence on Morrissey, Mark Stewart, and the Pet Shop Boys. The fact that he cost them a million bucks for no return whatsoever might have bugged the company's accountant, but from an artistic standpoint, how much more support could you ask for? Besides, what goes around comes around; five years later, the company clawed all that back and more to spare when it launched the Cars as the hottest group to come out of Boston all decade. And though many years, and a great deal of water, had flowed beneath the bridge since then, still Elektra possessed a maverick reputation, and one which instantly appealed to Phish.

"It just seems like the people there care about music and not just about business," Mike enthused. "They all seem to be very personable and easy to get along with." In stark contrast to many other artists' opinions of the labels to which they are bound, he smiled, "We really got the feeling that we were working together and not just against each other."

The proposed recording contract called for two new Phish albums, with an option for two more, "and two more after that," laughed Mike. "That's up to them, but usually bands don't even get two guaranteed at once. It means [Elektra] are more likely to promote the first one, since they are going to have to do a second one also." Again, that was an important distinction.

Another interesting aspect of the Elektra contract was that it also recognized Phish's constantly growing, and ever-inquisitive, fan base. Reissue rights for both *Junta* and *Lawn Boy* were included in the deal, with the label looking to unleash those packages within months of Phish's next new album.

There was one set of sacrifices, however, which Phish were forced to make. In an age when "complete creative control" was a contractual luxury which most bands could only dream of, and even then not feel certain they would ultimately be permitted, Phish accepted that their first album for Elektra would be subject to "mutual creative control," meaning that both parties were required to agree on the contents of the album.

They were initially loath to go along with that. It was not, after all, unheard of for a group to be completely redesigned once a clause like that got its claws in them, but Mike put a brave face on the situation regardless. "The thing is, it's unlikely that they are gonna say, 'You can't do this,' because it's not going to help anyone if it's a stalemate situation. I think they're going to be cooperative with what we do, and we're going to try to be cooperative too."

As if to prove the company's own good intentions, Elektra

even proved willing to budge over one issue which could have scuppered negotiations there and then, a second clause which insisted that the songs needed to be deemed "commercially satisfactory" by the label.

According to Mike, "Our lawyer didn't like the way that sounded, because it's possible that they could say, 'This isn't going to be a radio hit,' which it's definitely not going to be. So he had that word changed to 'technically satisfactory,' which is a big difference, because that just means that it's recorded well in the studio . . . not whether it's going to be [suitable for] the radio or not."

The contract covering subsequent albums did not make these same stipulations, but the label did reserve the right to choose the producer for the second album, and Mike acknowledged that "they are going to want to do certain [other] things." But, he continued, "it's really just a good situation because we have access to more resources in general, and they are not going to force a situation on us"—which was just as well, because much of Phish's new album was already in the can, the product of a few frenzied weeks at Burlington's White Crow Studios that summer. By the time the contract negotiations were finished, the album, *Picture of Nectar*, was complete.

Phish signed to Elektra on November 22, 1991. Almost a year of negotiations was required before the deal could be completed, and everybody was entitled to breathe a considerable sigh of relief once a finalized document could be laid on the table. Trey summed up a lot of people's feelings when he turned up for the final signing in a stupid wig, as if to say, That's got the bullshit out of the way; now, let's have some fun.

Picture of Nectar, as the sleeve notes made plain, was Phish's tribute to the Burlington bar where they played what they considered to be their first proper show. "We dedicate this album to Nectar Rorris for sixteen years of bringing Burlington live music every night of the week, with no cover and the best fries this side of . . . France." Nectar Rorris himself appears in silhouette on the album's sleeve.

The album comprised "mostly the stuff we've been playing over the past year a lot," Mike revealed in an online interview that November. That meant studio airings for the Gamehendge postscript "Llama," "Cavern," and "Tweezer" ("Memories" and "Runaway Jim" were also recorded, although they wouldn't make it to the album). Phish's first, and so far only, recorded cover version, a thirty-second snippet of Dizzy Gillespie's "Manteca," turned up, and there was even room for "The Mango Song," which had been waiting around since 1987 for recorded immortality.

And then there was "Faht," a song which started life under the highly expressive title of "Windham Hell," and went out of its way to parody every New Age nuance it could find. Unfortunately, lawyers representing the similarly named Windham Hill label, which does specialize in New Age–y material, objected strongly, and with the album sleeve just days away from going to the printers, Phish were asked to come up with an alternate title.

It was a tricky moment; not because they were especially fond of "Windham Hell," but because Fish was away on holiday, and his democratic input was essential to any decision they made. But there was no helping that now. The remaining trio set to work, only to find that inspiration was not too far away.

A few months earlier, penning a Phish update for the group's own *Doniac Schvice* newsletter service, Fish inadvertantly slipped in a typo, "faht" for "fast." No one else picked up on it until a couple of thousand mailings later, when the drummer was mortified to spot it in print.

The rest of Phish, of course, never let him forget it, but

the joke was getting old now. Maybe it was time to give it one last airing, and then retire it forever. Fish returned from vacation to be assured that he wasn't the only person who could make embarrassing typographical slips. "I don't know how it happened," Trey told him, "but Elektra let one through on the album sleeve. Look how they spelled 'Windham Hell'— 'F-A-H-T.' "

Musically, *Picture of Nectar* was a considerably more structured album than either of its predecessors. Mike championed, "I think we've been moving in the direction of having songs be more focused, whereas on *Junta* they were long and patched-together type songs. And the last album was sort of slightly shorter songs that are a little bit more concise. This album doesn't have any big epic-type songs."

Okay, he conceded, so "Tweezer" approached nine minutes, and "Stash" topped seven. But the vast majority were under five minutes, and a few weighed in under three. Compared to the lush horizons of its predecessors, *Picture of Nectar* was a veritable radio-friendly unit shifter. Nor was that a conscious decision on the part of the band—or the label. "It just sort of happened that way."

At the same time, however, Mike admitted that there was some sound commercial sense to including shorter songs. Tacitly confessing that some of Elektra's concerns did filter through to Phish's own line of thought, "Radio usually only plays songs that are less than four or five minutes, and none of our [older] songs are less than four or five minutes. So it's not often that some song will fit that category." And though radio play was not the most important item on Phish's To Do list, it was a consideration. After all, if part of the purpose of making an album is to let people hear your songs, it doesn't matter whether they're in a listening booth in their favorite record store, or steaming down the highway on their way home from work, with the radio blaring around them. Elektra even chose a single from the disc, the breezy "Chalk Dust Torture."

There were other considerations, however, which went into shaping the eventual nature of *Picture of Nectar*. "With the first album," Mike remembered, "people said we sounded too much like our influences." As they set about preparing *Picture of Nectar*, Phish made a conscious decision that, instead of continuing to develop their original sound, each song would instead become an exploration "of a certain kind of music or genre."

The end result, Mike insisted while the sessions were still under way, would be "very diverse. There's one song of every kind of music on it—jazz, country, Irish, funk, rock, reggae, Latin, you name it.

"It's funny, we always want to make an album that's more narrow stylistically, but it always ends up in an opposite direction. Suddenly we had a jazz song, a bluegrass tune, a funk number, and we did not even realize it was going to come out that way."

Such eclecticism, of course, served a number of purposes, not only offering a showcase for each group member's own personal influences, but also defying any passing critic to simply fasten on to one prevalent sound and pigeonhole Phish before they'd even been heard.

"There's no way we could play a country song as well as a country band, or a Latin song as well as a Latin band," Mike admitted, but that wasn't the point. The point was to establish a broad range of musical parameters within which Phish could reasonably work." He joked to the *Washington Post* in 1993, "Rock, jazz, Broadway, funk, bluegrass, and Latin, those are our influences. We used to list twelve, but we whittled it down to six. We lost hardcore, calypso, reggae, blues, and some others." What he really meant, of course, was that Phish was consciously trying to pull away from those endless Dead comparisons.

Time and experience alone would tell whether those wishes were to come true. In the meantime, so pervasive were the Phish/Dead comparisons that one of Elektra's first actions was to address the magazines most commonly associated with the Deadhead community—*Relix, Unbroken Chain*, and *Dupree's Diamond News*—not quite forbidding but certainly discouraging them from talking to the group.

Of course it didn't make too much difference; even today, those magazines remain Phish's closest, and most valued, link with the newsstands. But *Unbroken Chain* at least would accompany one Phish feature with the lament, "This will probably be [this magazine's] last in-depth Phish interview because Phish's record company/publicity department has made it abundantly clear that they don't want to be in a Dead publication. I think," editor Laura Paul Smith wrote, "you can understand why."

Indeed one could. It is natural for critics to compare one band with another, if only to give the reader a convenient peg upon which to hang a new talent—one cannot, after all, describe every group as absolutely unique! But for Phish, the Dead comparisons were not only tiring, they were tired as well, particularly once they moved away from the world of fanspeak and computer networks, and into the pages of the national media.

In March 1993, *Entertainment Weekly* became one of the first mainstream publications to seriously profile Phish. But even this generally sympathetic article would appear beneath the headline "Jerry's Kids"; would joke about tie-dyed shirts and free-form solos; and would continue with a remark about being told by your parents about bands like this . . . "and now we have our own, man!" Phish, writer David Browne chortled, "is even better than that Dead cover band that plays here every Wednesday."

Fish continues to recognize the similarities in form and format between Phish and the Dead. "We both jam a lot," for example. And he agreed that the Dead "were one of the rock bands in America that had a sense of group improvisation. [But] they had more of a folk and bluegrass overall feel . . . I don't think they had as much Latin and calypso, or some of the weirder stuff. I think musically the bands are pretty different." Plus, he laughed, "their lyrics made sense."

"When we are at our best," Mike continued, "we definitely do things that the Dead or no other band could do. We explore things and take things to the extreme. For example, jams sometimes turn into really different sounding things. Like the drumbeat will change, or the chord progression will change, that sort of thing. Sometimes it will develop into something really specific that we've never played before. That's something that even jazz bands don't do too much. . . . I mean, they improvise all the time, but we try to change the structure sometimes." And then he told interviewer (and future Dionysian Productions staffer) Shelly Culbertson, "I'm not really allowed to talk about the Dead."

Yet it was hard, sometimes, for copy-hungry journalists to draw the fine distinctions which Phish's music unquestionably deserved. There were just too many other parallels to be made, and by the end of 1991, yet another would raise its head, as the unity which bound Phish to their ever-swelling audience leaped into the computer age with the birth of the Phish Net.

The Deadhead network was one of the first fan bases to realize the potential of the Internet, painstakingly organizing itself in deepest cyberspace, all the better to trade tapes and set-lists, cadge lifts to gigs, and just keep in touch. Matt Laurence, a computer-graphics designer from Hamilton,

Massachusetts, was just one of the myriad people who logged on to the newsgroup, to see what was going on; he was one of the first, however, to notice there was something missing from the communications. "I had been a Phish fan for quite a while, [when] I noticed that nobody had really heard of Phish in the computer newsgroups that I watched, except, that is, for a very few people on the Grateful Dead network. Eventually I noticed that the number of people writing about Phish on the Grateful Dead network was growing, and I thought, 'Why not a Phish network?' I decided to call it Phish Net." The first postings appeared on this precocious entity on August 27, 1991, and by the end of the year, over three hundred subscribers regularly corresponded.

The Phish Net was originally established without any official go-ahead from the group themselves. It was not long, however, before they became involved, not only contributing to its pages, but also using it as a conduit for information, from Phish to fan, and back again.

"The Phish Net really changed the face of the band," Trey admitted, "because anytime anything happens that's out of the ordinary—which is pretty much every Phish concert, everybody on the network knows about it the next night." One of his favorite examples was the night Phish debuted six songs in one show. By morning, the Phish Net not only included descriptions of the songs, but also details on how fans could get tapes of them.

"So within days, you've got tapes of these new songs all over the country, which is exactly what we'd want. That way, when we go out on [our next] national tour, people are going to have heard of the new songs, and even have tapes of the new songs, before we get to different towns." By 1993, Phish themselves were supplying the Phish Net with tapes, for downloading by subscribers. Some of the greatest Phish shows of the period would attain mass circulation in this fashion.

Of course, it was not long before news of the Phish Net began to leak into the mainstream media; the existence of such a well-organized—some might even say fanatical—fan base would have been newsworthy whatever group it followed. The fact that Phish themselves were next to unknown only heightened the curiosity.

Not that Phish were likely to remain undercover for long.

Phish concluded their 1991 touring schedule with their now-traditional New Year's Eve performance in Boston. That was the night Chris Kuroda remembers as the moment he realized Phish were getting big . . . very big. "For me, along the way there were a few, but the big one that I remember just knocking my socks off was New Year's at Worcester Memorial Auditorium. And it was just, 'Wow, this place is huge!' "

Close to four thousand fans paid $16.50 a head to pack the Auditorium, a seething mass which poured through the doors to be greeted by a staggering sight, a massive canvas backdrop painted by Mike's mother, Marjorie Minkin. Phish were playing three full sets that night, with the New Year countdown falling smack in the middle of the second set, and the third turning into one of the longest and most dramatic jams in the band's history, gliding seamlessly through "Wilson," "The Squirming Coil," "Tweezer," "McGrupp," "Mike's Song," and "I Am Hydrogen," before finally crashing ashore with "Weekapaug Groove."

But the show didn't simply ring out the old year with a sizable bang, it got the new one off to a pretty good start as well. The following day, Boston's number one FM radio station, WBCN, broadcast the entire concert over the air. Throughout the station's catchment area, the tapes were rolling with a vengeance that day!

Storming into the new year, an appearance on National Public Radio's *Mountain Stage Live* program did even more to heighten Phish's profile; so did the release of *Picture of Nectar* to bemused reviews but strong initial sales—35,000 is not many copies by mainstream rock standards, but Elektra, at least, was delighted. The reissue of *Lawn Boy* was set for July; a bonus track–packed *Junta* would follow in November. With their label obviously doing so much for the band, it was natural that the media would want to get in early as well.

By the time Phish's spring 1992 tour was under way, Phish Net creator Mark Laurence had given several interviews, while a number of other newspapers had run respectably sizable previews of upcoming Phish shows. And no less an authority than the *New Yorker* was asking Trey to detail an average week in this "maddeningly eclectic" but loyally supported group's life.

He sounded weary, cynical even, but he also knew it was worth the pain. "I think our music and shows are fun to talk about. People talk about sex a lot, and music is similar. It's this thing that is so powerful. It's about communication, so people are fascinated by it. And you can't ever really put your finger on it. Music moves people"—and it moves them to do some very bizarre things. Things like "play until two, get to the hotel by four, sleep eight hours, and get woken by the maids"—and then get thrashed at football by the road crew.

Chris Kuroda remembers, "We used to play football on the beach and the crew used to crush them all the time. So the band forced us to play hockey, because Trey's a great hockey player and [so is] John Paluska. So we were out there basically falling down, toes pointed in at each other, and these guys were just having a field day with us. The whole reason was that we beat them so many times at football, they just couldn't take it anymore."

Weighted victories over their crew notwithstanding, the road, Mike detailed, "has its pros and cons. The con is that we miss our loved ones at home. The pro is that it is the most incredible thing in the world, even more than people think. This groove gets started, like cycles in the day. We play five nights a week, we become comfortable playing, we build up a stamina and then we open ourselves up to let anything happen in these cycles. By being somewhat routined by the road, it can actually feel free and that brings security. I just have to take a deep breath and remember that it can be more fun than anyone ever imagined."

Or it can be even more infuriating than that. On March 21, 1992, Phish played one of those shows where, for Chris Kuroda at least, everything that could go wrong did. Plugging in Kuroda's lights that night, Paul Languedoc inadvertently tied into 220 watts instead of 110. "He fried the light show," Kuroda recalled, "just fried the dimmer rack." The lights themselves survived their ordeal, so Phish suggested Kuroda simply work them one light at a time. "Take the lights off the light rig, and plug them into the wall and slowly, throughout the night, build a lighting collage."

"I didn't want to do that," Kuroda admits, "but I didn't have a choice. Something had to happen. So I started building my lighting collage, putting lights on the piano, but it wasn't really working out so they said, 'Just do stuff, whatever.'"

Kuroda obliged, and the night ended, he recalls, with him bouncing up and down on Trey's trampoline, holding a light over the guitarist while he continued to play. "It was just a night I don't like to remember that much!"

Phish's spring 1992 tour, their first under the auspices of Elektra, was their first not to be reliant upon the college-campus circuit; rather, the band was hitting small theaters and large clubs, seldom appearing in front of less than a thousand people a night. Yet even this advance could not have prepared them for their next step, a summer spent acquainting themselves with America's sprawling stadium circuit.

H.O.R.D.E.—Horizons of Rock Developing Everywhere—started small, a long way from the "neo-hippie Lollapalooza" which some critics have dubbed more recent excursions, and certainly not something which the participants ever dreamed would swiftly become an integral part of the 1990s rock circuit. When it was first conceived, in the Manhattan offices of Bill Graham Presents, that Valentine's morning in 1992, it was, as Bruce Hampton remembered, simply a good idea.

"We all flew in. . . . We tried to keep it as idealistic as possible. No management, no booking agent, just the bands. It was Phish, Blues Traveler, Widespread Panic, and myself for the Aquarium Rescue Unit. The bands did not have huge followings at the time, so we said, 'Let's put them together.' "

That H.O.R.D.E. would later be compared to Lollapalooza, in terms of presentation if not media impact, was of course inevitable; Perry Farrell's little monster had already all but copyrighted the idea of sticking piles of bands on buses and then driving them around the country. What was more surprising was that in terms of integrity, H.O.R.D.E. would so outstrip Lollapalooza, that long after a voracious mainstream subverted Farrell's original ideas and idealism, H.O.R.D.E. would continue traveling incognito, selling out venues, but never its principles.

For the first two years of its existence, H.O.R.D.E. was self-produced by Blues Traveler. Not until 1994 did the big-business acumen of Bill Graham Presents wade in; it would be two years more before Cellar Door Productions threw their hat into the ring as well, and Heidi Kelso, one of H.O.R.D.E.'s original organizers, was justifiably proud when she told *Relix*, "The greatest thing about the H.O.R.D.E.

since the beginning is that it sort of created its own thing. We didn't have corporate sponsorship and nobody really directed the course of the way this tour has grown. Everybody's really proud of what it has become, and people seem to like it, even though it has become a lot bigger." Even with the 1996 entourage of three major headline attractions, forty-five support groups, three stages, a dozen buses, six tractor trailers, a fifty-strong production crew, and forty-two venues bursting at the seams with fans, she enthused, "I don't think the original elements that made it special have been lost."

The very premise of H.O.R.D.E., of course, dictated a Dream Team lineup: Blues Traveler, Widespread Panic, Colonel Bruce Hampton and the Aquarium Rescue Unit, Spin Doctors, and either banjo maestro Bela Fleck or Phish, depending upon which end of the tour one caught. Phish were booked for the closing salvo. Although the acronym's full title spelled out the basic intentions of the participating bands, to take what passes for rock 'n' roll to its outermost limits, the very nature of rock in the 1990s demanded a certain streamlining—even Lollapalooza fell prey to that. "[But] while it's easy to label these as neo-retro hippie rock," *Guitar Player*'s Mike Mettler wrote reassuringly, "they've all just released albums that solidify their individual identities and signal a clear transition from formula rock back to free-form rock."

Trey pursued the author's train of thought, insisting, "musically we're very different," illustrating that point by recalling the first time Phish ever jammed with Fleck's outfit—which also happened to be the first time they'd ever met them. "We decided to get everybody up onstage and just go for it. We did that for an hour. It was wild. Some of it was bad. Some of it was great." But all of it worked, in the true spirit of making music, which left it to *Guitar Player* magazine's Mike Mettler to emphasize, "The common thread binding the H.O.R.D.E. is that . . . all of these bands love to be onstage for lo-o-o-o-ng sets. They're uninterested in faithful note-for-note reproduction of a three-minute single, a few don't even play songs less than five minutes long, and some have a thing or two about lengthy sets and improvisation."

Trey agreed. "Rock 'n' roll is about blasting energy. It's basically a volume thing. But there's also an unexplored world of harmony out there just waiting to explode." He damned the attitude which arose with the punk movement of the late 1970s, and has hamstringed attempts at musical progression ever since—the pernicious belief that "if you know too much about theory or the history of music, then you're not playing rock 'n' roll."

He knew, and hoped others did too, that this catch-all condemnation, in its widespread acceptance through the 1980s and early 1990s, overlooked the fact that it's not technique which makes great music, it's attitude. The most proficient musician in the world, it is true, might not be a great rock 'n' roller, and vice versa. But that is not because he can (or can't) play his instrument, it is because he cannot play it with the unbridled passion, and the indefinable soul, which is, after all, what rock 'n' roll is all about.

That was the point which H.O.R.D.E. intended bringing home, and it was, *Rolling Stone* journalist Jeff Giles opined, "about time. For the last few years, [these] jam-happy bands . . . with little record-company support . . . have been sparking grassroots followings wherever tapes are taped then taped again. The bands are playing different sets every night, nearly two hundred nights a year. They're doing what the Spin Doctors' frontman, Chris Barron, always wanted to do: 'Play the gig, blow everybody's mind, and make music that's music.' "

For much of the vast readership which *Rolling Stone* commands, Giles's examination of H.O.R.D.E. would be their first encounter with Phish and Company. But if they followed their hearts and caught one of the shows, it would not be their last. "Twenty years ago," Giles wrote, "this article would have been about Little Feat and Hot Tuna . . . the Allmans and the Dead."

The H.O.R.D.E. crowd, after all, already reveled in their underground connections. Blues Traveler's manager, David Graham, was the son of the late legendary San Francisco promoter Bill Graham, and until his death in a helicopter crash in 1991, Graham was the one American entrepreneur to have so surpassed his milieu that he could have put himself onstage and still sold out a stadium.

Then there was the much-vaunted camaraderie which bound the H.O.R.D.E. bands and fans as closely as the Dead, the Airplane, Quicksilver, and the like were linked a quarter of a century before, in the public perception at least.

Trey reinforced this when he spoke of "a similarity in attitude between the H.O.R.D.E. bands, family orientation with your crew and your audience, a focus on playing live." But it was writer Giles who brought the point home most forcibly, when he described the events of March 14, 1992, when Phish headlined New York City's cavernous Roseland Ballroom. They did not even need to introduce John Popper to the assembled masses when he strode out onstage; the crowd knew him on sight and roared their own welcome as he joined Phish through a burning rendition of "Good Times Bad Times."

The Roseland show was fabulous, one of the best Phish had played in New York since they graduated from the Wetlands Preserve, and *Rolling Stone* was not the only national publication to be paying attention. Outside, *High Times* writer Nate Eaton described encountering "a mass of people . . . freshman orientation day at the Jerry Garcia State University," punctuated by the ticketless miraclers, hoping against hope, but trusting all the same, that someone might spare them the price of admission. I NEED A MIRACLE PLEASE, begged one; SOMEONE PLEASE DOSE ME WITH A PHISH TICKET, pleaded another.

And Eaton, a self-confessed novice in a sea of seasoned pros, listened spellbound while a pair of Burlington boys discussed the two-hundred-foot line which snaked down the street, and the stampede for tickets that left so many fans out in the cold. "I had no idea it would get this big," groaned one. "Yeah," replied his buddy, and he looked around—"this is nuts!"

It was, as well. It was utterly nuts as the invasion of Newbies, brand-new Phish fans descending en masse, made it impossible for the older fans to get a ticket for shows. Every time the group hit a different city now, the Phish Net rang with the fans' indignation, and their scornful put-downs of the moms and dads with an armful of kids, setting out their picnic hamper in the center of the room.

It was as if the Dead crowd, pushed out of their own season-ticketed roosts by an invasion of their own turf, had decided to do the same thing to someone else, and though the Internet chat rooms would blaze with contradiction, there was some truth to it. For the last three evenings, the Dead were playing at Nassau Coliseum, and more than a few fans stayed in town for the Phish gig, confident that whatever vibes they'd picked up at one show would still be around at the next. The Dead were big and getting bigger, and the overflow needed to go somewhere. What could be more natural, then, than for the exiled fans to flick through *Dupree's*, and go see the first band they found profiled within?

Not everybody was put off by the burgeoning Phish experience. *Rolling Stone* tracked down some of the more optimistic souls at a Blues Traveler gig at Wetlands, shortly before the H.O.R.D.E. tour kicked off. "I was a Deadhead for years," one twenty-year-old revealed. "But that whole scene's been ruined for me. There's all these burnt-out hippie scumbags exploiting everybody and selling drugs that aren't even any fucking good."

Bands like Spin Doctors, Phish, and Blues Traveler offered an alternative to that scene, one in which "everybody's your own age and you don't have to worry about getting mugged. And they do these totally sick jam sessions that are perfect for acid." Now, she considered herself "a tourhead," and she was not alone. The thing was, how long could this new scene exist before it, too, fell prey to those same burnt-out hippie scumbags?

Where there's a crowd, there are the people who are attracted by crowds, the roistering hooligans who don't care who's playing, just so long as there's a good time waiting to be had. "It's already gotten too big," one old-school Phish fan told a *New York Times* reporter. "You get more kinds of people at concerts. There are the tourheads, but there are also the frat guys who don't like us. I don't know how much bigger it can get and still survive."

Phish tried not to become drawn into these arguments, but they found themselves responding anyway. Mike, in particular, was embroiled in a succession of Internet arguments, discussing the size to which Phish was capable of growing, and trying to assure fans that big is not always bad.

Following his reasoned, reasonable line of thinking, one began to question the nature of a "real fan," aside from someone sad enough to have supported the same band for longer than is healthy, to have bunkered themselves in with a sports-supporter mentality, until gigs became statistics which they could chalk up on the bedpost, and what should have been magical became simply routine.

There are Phish Heads out there who've loved their group longer than they've loved their own families; who'd readily forget an anniversary, but can still remember the first time they saw their heroes onstage; who would, forced to choose between one and the other, happily face a life alone, so long as that 4/5/90 J. J. McCabe's tape was playing in the background.

Yet these are often the same people who can speak passionately against government attempts to impose morality by law, or religions which have no tolerance for other beliefs. It is a dilemma which Jerry Garcia chose to treat with silence— as one observer put it, "If I was put into Jerry Garcia's position, where so many 'faithful' waited for my next utterance for their life's guidance, I probably wouldn't say much either. Or I'd shoot heroin."

If the press reports are to be believed, it was precisely that kind of audience at Roseland. And if it was that hectic for one group, who could say what would happen with five of them on display?

NOT EVERYONE IN THE LOT IS YOUR FRIEND

The H.O.R.D.E. tour was short—four shows in the North-east, four in the South; Phish's part in the affair was even shorter. Returning to America from an eight-date visit to west-ern Europe, hitting Continental festivals and bizarre double bills with the likes of the Violent Femmes, Phish appeared at just four H.O.R.D.E. shows: in Portland, Maine; Syracuse, New York; Holmdel, New Jersey; and Jones Beach, New York, between July 9 and 12, 1992. From there, there would just be time to sneak in a few shows on their own, and then it was back on the bus as special guests of Santana.

But it was not the fact they'd be playing almost thirty shows, in stadium-sized venues, in under six weeks, that most impressed Phish. It was the chance to perform with one of their own idols, and one of the genuine legends of rock 'n' roll.

Tijuana-born Carlos Santana's stylish fusion of Latin rhythms within a rock framework emerged out of the same San Francisco scene that spawned the Dead, the Airplane, and all the other customary suspects. But like Creedence Clearwater Revival, another outfit who called the late-sixties

Bay Area home, Santana was part of that movement by geographical, and maybe chemical, circumstance alone. Musically, Santana offered little in common with what their neighbors were playing, plowing instead a personal groove which was as individual as it was infectious, and as impermeable, too. Musical and personal ruptures came and went, but Santana's vision remained undeflected, undeflectable.

Not even the massive fame that descended upon the group in the early 1970s, after they stole the show at the Woodstock Festival, was allowed to distract the group. Or maybe it did a little, as they slipped into the megarock routine of triple live albums with exploding gatefold covers, and weighty pronouncements about God, love, and life. For a while there, Santana did lose the musical plot, sinking into a kind of complacency even as their audience's expectations settled into the same comfortable routine that Santana, his guitar-hero credentials now inviolate, too often locked into his playing.

But maybe that was for the best after all, because when the headline hustlers started hunting elsewhere, Santana regained the magic and the muse, and though some media mavens called this latest tour a comeback, it was they who were coming back to the fold, not Santana.

"It's important to connect to people's hearts something that's not even of me, but through me," Santana explained in 1994, looking back over more than a quarter century spent making his music. "My own heart goes out to people who say, 'Hey, I don't feel so good about this planet. Instead of doing what my mom and dad did, which was dedicate their lives to being richer and richer, I want to go down to El Salvador and teach those people how to dig a well.' Those people are my heroes today. My heroes are not musicians anymore."

Trey was unswerved. "Carlos Santana has always been a

hero of mine," he gushed. When he was seven, he recalled, his parents would sit down with the Woodstock triple live album, and it was always Santana's contribution, the epic "Soul Sacrifice," which grabbed the boy's attention—would, in fact, become "one of the reasons I started playing music. And here we are twenty years later, and Carlos is still going with the right ideas. He's not in it for the money, he's just an incredible guy."

Later, looking back on the tour with writer Paul Semel, a fan of Phish since he first caught them at college, Trey continued, "There was something about standing there with him every night for six weeks. He'd play a solo, and I'd play a solo. The learning was incredible, just to be there with him and picking up the vibe. With him, you felt it was just pouring out of him, right out of his heart, through his guitar into the crowd."

The feelings were evidently mutual. Talking with Santana after one show, Trey was stunned when the master began singing Phish's praises as loudly as they sang his. "He said that when he was listening to us, he envisioned the audience as a sea of flowers. The music was the water, and we were the hose. He said that the music is basically there. Musicians are the vehicle."

Later, out surfing on the Pacific, Trey found himself with more time to digest Santana's words. "If you're surfing, you can't fight the ocean. The wave is coming and it's a lot stronger than you. If you relax, have no fear, and you're with the flow of the wave, then you're going to be able to surf. If you try to fight it, you can't ride it. The same wave can be a source of incredible pain or beautiful flowing grace, depending on how you deal with it.

"It's the same thing with live music to me. If you can let go of everything, it can be the most uplifting, enlightening, beautiful, charging experience. When that's happening, you feel that you can do no wrong. The notes are just pouring out and you couldn't stop it if you wanted to."

In the months to come, sharp ears would be readily able to discern precisely the impact Santana exerted on Phish, the "samba-ish quality to parts of 'Rift' and 'Maze,' " which *Relix* magazine pointed out; guitar sounds which reflected Santana's own; Hammond organ effects which recalled Greg Rolie's timeless B3. In the meantime, it was thrilling enough for Phish simply to be able to jam with Santana. They could worry about absorbing all they were learning later on.

"It's great," Mike rhapsodized. "The best thing is when the music really just sort of takes off and goes its own way. That is the single best part of the experience."

On October 30, 1992, Phish played Boston radio station WBCN's New Music Concert, a reunion of sorts with H.O.R.D.E.-mates Spin Doctors, but one which took place under very different circumstances to their last onstage pairing.

Six months earlier, as the H.O.R.D.E. tour was coming together, the Spin Doctors' debut album had racked up modest sales of around 60,000. Then WEQX out of Vermont picked up on the band's latest single, MTV grabbed on to their recent video releases, and *A Pocketful of Kryptonite* was now selling through the roof.

Suddenly, everything anyone ever dreamed might happen to Phish was vindicated. Without ever stepping out of the confines they had erected around their music, Spin Doctors were ineffable evidence that you could grasp mainstream success without relinquishing your hold on underground credibility. Yet it was not the headlining Spin Doctors who grabbed the next day's headlines. It was Phish.

WBCN's Oedipus remembers, "Phish was booked to play our annual 'Rock of Boston' charity concert at the Boston Garden, and as I recall, the Phish 'Rock of Boston' was the only one to sell out completely. I was amazed at the passion and strength of their following."

That passion would become even more pronounced following the release of Phish's fourth album, *Rift*. Within weeks of its February 1993 release, the record was soaring to number 7 on the local album chart. Later, *Picture of Nectar* would be voted Best Major Label Debut of 1992 at the annual Boston Music Awards.

True to their word, Elektra opted to pair Phish with a producer of the company's own choice for what would become *Rift*. Although the self-produced *Picture of Nectar* had at least fulfilled expectations, there was a growing conviction in the record-company hierarchy that with a live support as large as theirs, Phish ought to be exceeding expectations. A seasoned hand at the controls was the first step toward achieving that.

All the same, Barry Beckett was an unusual choice. Over the years, the pianist and arranger had worked successfully with acts as disparate as Aretha Franklin and Dire Straits, while his partnership with Jerry Wexler was also responsible for two of the most divisive (but sonically impeccable) albums in Bob Dylan's entire career, the *Slow Train Coming* and *Saved* discs which introduced the erstwhile iconoclast's newfound Christianity to a stunned world. Lyrically, many of Dylan's fans were repulsed by their idol's latest direction, but none could fault the apocalyptic arrangements that Beckett brought into play.

Yet from the moment the sessions kicked off at White Crow Studios in Burlington, in September 1992, Phish insisted that they were in control; the very choice of studios was a sign of their autonomy, while they also opted to choose their own engineer, Kevin Halprin, rather than bring in one of Beckett's acolytes.

Despite these differences, the Beckett-Phish team proved instantly compatible, not necessarily because they understood each other, but because both parties understood what they were trying to do. "He's our soul gauge," Trey confessed. "He has an incredible ear for groove and for soul."

Beckett, for example, simply smiled when Phish announced that they intended issuing an open invitation on local radio, for anyone who wanted to sing on the album to make their way down to the studio immediately. The assembled gathering of freaks, fans, and the vaguely curious would be immortalized on the group sing-along which closes the album.

Phish, meanwhile, could not do anything but smile when Beckett listened to a rough playback of Tom Marshall's "Fast Enough for You," and then remarked, "this might come on the radio after an Eric Clapton song."

"We replied, 'Ohhhh,' " Trey recalled. He could remember the first time he heard Clapton's lament for his recently deceased young son, "Tears in Heaven"; the way the song's open-sore sentimentality "just blew me away," and it took him a moment to realize that with "Fast Enough for You," Tom struck a similar raw, emotional note. Many of Marshall's contributions to the new album were dominated by recent events in the lyricist's personal life, but "Fast Enough for You" went straight to their heart, an almost painstaking examination of the conflict between maintaining a relationship and maintaining your own sanity.

"We had never touched on that kind of direct emotion on our other records," Trey continued. By the time this most naked of songs was complete, "I think [it] threw a lot of people for a loop." But he couldn't resist throwing one sly little in-joke into the brew, a long, pining outro which was straight out of the Clapton songbook.

"That Clapton thing was still in my mind," Trey admitted, "especially his fade-out on 'Let It Grow' (from the *461 Ocean Boulevard* album), which kind of spins backwards into the void of emptiness. I wanted ours to drift off like it did."

And Beckett's own initial instinct was eventually proven correct. "Fast Enough for You" became the first single to be culled from *Rift*, and at least one Adult Contemporary radio DJ did spin it after Eric Clapton.

Rift was released in early February 1993. A week before it hit the stores, however, on January 28, 1993, Boston's Hard Rock Cafe hosted the album's release party.

It was a moving occasion. Beneath walls festooned with the debris of thirty years of rock 'n' roll memorabilia, Fish offered his own gift to the Cafe's collection, the 1967 Electrolux vacuum cleaner which appeared on the cover of *Lawn Boy*. It was the first one he'd ever played onstage.

Phish themselves regaled the masses with just one song that evening. For the last few months, they'd been taking lessons in the gentle art of barbershop-quartet singing, and there could be no better occasion than this to air their newfound talents. Hushing the revelers, Phish launched into an amazing a cappella "Amazing Grace."

Rift was released a week later, just as Phish's spring tour got under way on February 3, 1993, at the Expo, in Portland, Maine. Page's latest acquisition, a baby grand piano, made its debut that night, causing the band's ever-suffering road crew a whole new set of headaches as he fussed around it, making sure that it looked as shiny and new at the end of the day as it appeared when he bought it. At a time when most groups were downscaling their keyboard arsenals, slaves to the electronic minimalism of contemporary fashion, it was typical of Phish to start enlarging theirs.

Such onstage grandiosity, of course, was the welcome face of Phish's burgeoning popularity. A less agreeable side to their success also made its appearance on this tour, however, and unlike the baby grand, it didn't matter how it was treated, it would bounce back unharmed the next evening.

It is a law of human nature that when demand for a commodity outstrips supply, somebody will try and step into the breach. In the music industry, bootleg recordings are one totally harmless example of this, as free enterprise seeks to sate an appetite which private enterprise is incapable of meeting. Counterfeit tickets, on the other hand, benefit nobody except their manufacturers; few, if any, of the venues where such deceptions pose a danger are equipped with the latest in forgery detection equipment, and as the Phish road show began moving down the coast, the rip-off merchants swung into action.

Of course, Phish were not the counterfeiters' only target on the tour circuit, but there was something about the group's fan base, their trusting nature, maybe, or the belief that they were all in this together, which made them that much easier targets. "Remember," countless editorials in *Relix* warned, "not everyone in the parking lot is your friend." Unfortunately, that warning came too late for too many luckless, ticketless, and now moneyless fans.

Phish were powerless to halt the rip-off. Warnings were posted on the Phish Net, and security teams were briefed to keep scalpers at bay, but the problem did not go away; rather, it simply grew, as hardened ticket touts simply adopted the same costume as their intended victims, and sank to the same depths of undercover deception as the police teams who were also, suddenly, beginning to target Phish audiences. For the hapless Phish freak, miracling for tickets and on the lookout for a high, parking lots were turning into shooting galleries. You never knew who you could trust.

Some of Phish's best-loved later songs made their debut on
the 1993 spring tour: the whacked-out "Sample in a Jar,"
"The Wedge," "Lifeboy," and a rolling cover of the Rolling
Stones' "Loving Cup" all appeared during the earliest shows.
Later gigs introduced "Pig in a Pen," "Nellie Cane," "It's My
Life," and an audacious take on Pink Floyd's near-
instrumental "Great Gig in the Sky"—audacious because no
live group, not even Pink Floyd themselves, ever truly recap-
tured the sheer emotive majesty of that most evocative of
workouts. Many of these were already in place when Phish
reached New York, for two nights at the Roseland Ballroom,
just three days into the tour.

Neither show was a "normal" one. From the moment
"Llama" opened the first night, Phish played like musicians
possessed. But it was the following evening which lives on in
the memory: First when John Popper walked on for one of
his own now-regular guest spots; then for the encore, when
the band was joined by one of the men who made their next
song happen in the first place, Noel Redding, the bass player
on Jimi Hendrix's original recording of "Fire." In truth, his
contributions to the song were not impressively audible, but
that wasn't the point. For the watching masses, it was enough
simply to see another living legend confer his blessing, and
approval, upon Phish.

Phish's capacity for improvisation was to be stretched
to its limit as the tour wound on. In Knoxville, Tennessee,
the Electric Ballroom soundboard shorted out during
"Mound," a little over midway through the second set.
The group launched into an impromptu a capella "Amazing Grace" while the crew struggled to fix the board.
When a swift repair turned out to be impossible, the band
then carried on through "Memories" (from the musical
Cats), "Sweet Adeline," and "Mound," as though mixing

boards, electricity itself, were luxuries they really could live without.

A couple of nights later, Phish's own internal unpredictability swung into focus when Trey mischievously decided the only song he wanted to play through the second set was "Tweezer." No matter what the rest of the band attempted, be it the James Gang's "Walk Away," KISS's "Rock 'n' Roll All Night," or Mike's own "Mike's Song," Trey would return to the "Tweezer" theme whenever he could.

Futher confusion was sown for Phish's road crew, as the band swirled from auditorium to theater and back again. Chris Kuroda complained, "It drives me nuts. It's hard because you're always adapting. You just can't fit a huge light show in a small room, so you have to break it down, take parts out, squish it.

"But everything's planned out, cable lengths are exact, all cables are bundled together, every breakout from a cable is exactly as long as it needs to be. So when you start taking pieces away or changing shapes, now the cables don't reach. Also, lights remember where they're supposed to be from night to night, but now light number one, which is over here not over here, its idea of where Page is, is going to be at the ceiling. And the amount of updating . . . we're updating until the doors open. Sometimes even while people are inside, we're trying to get it going." Not until the end of the night could he sit back, relax, and reflect that it was worth it. "You go through all this hell all day, and by the time the show's going on and you look around and everybody's having a great time, you get a satisfaction. 'Okay, it was worth going through that hell.' "

Less worthwhile were the negotiations which had embroiled John Paluska's time almost since the tour was announced, but which weren't resolved until virtually the last minute, just days before Phish took the stage for their March 27 show at San Francisco's Warfield Theater.

MTV, the music video network that revolutionized American listening habits, had kept Phish very much at arm's length over the years, a state of affairs which wasn't helped by the band's refusal to give in to Elektra's request that they make a video. Now it seemed that Phish's instincts were correct. Mohammed had refused to go the mountain; so the mountain was going to go to him.

Twice during 1992, Phish appeared on MTV, first when "The Landlady" sprang up as background music to an episode of model Cindy Crawford's *House of Style* show; then, in July, when Phish turned up as the house band on *Hangin' with MTV*, treating viewers to a few seconds of "Divided Sky" and a brief vacuum solo before the cameras turned to less perplexing themes. Now MTV wanted to broadcast a full hour of Phish in concert.

Trey reflected, "We were almost going to do an MTV concert. They were going to film [us at] the Warfield, and that got to the point where we even met with the potential director. But then it disappeared, probably because the album didn't do so well." The cameras missed a killer show, but it was MTV's audience which suffered more. The cable music channel's anodyne output of *Unplugged* specials and unhinged superstars would certainly have benefited from a night spent with Phish.

The tour rolled on, through California and up the West Coast. It was halfway through that leg, in Portland, Oregon, on April 1, 1993, that Phish played one of the few political benefit concerts of their career, agreeing to turn out for the endangered ancient forest growth of the Pacific Northwest.

Although they have rarely been tarred with any shade of political brush, Fish at least acknowledges that because Phish "have some recognition, we have a certain responsibility for doing something, just in what we support. In our organization, we have money that we set aside for charity. A certain percentage goes to two specific things we support in Vermont: one is cleaning up Lake Champlain, the other is the King Street youth center where kids who hang out in the street can get support."

At the same time, Phish was wary of becoming involved in specific political events. Even though they were unequivocal in their support, for example, they turned down an invitation to play a benefit for a Vermont congressman, for fear of encouraging impressionable fans to make political decisions which they might not fully believe in, simply because Phish endorsed the candidate.

The ancient growth, though, was different. Fish believes that "supporting a single person, a political candidate, is very different than doing a gig for the rain forest or something that everybody shares." And besides, the ancient-forest-growth benefit sounded as though it was going to be very low-key indeed,

The show was taking place just hours before Phish were to play the local Roseland Theater, and Trey remembers, "[The organizers] said it was going to be on the green, there was going to be some other bands there, and they offered to get us some equipment. I said, 'Don't even get us any equipment. We'll do the whole thing a cappella.' I thought that would be cool. We'd never done that before." He laughs at his naïveté. "I was only expecting two hundred people to turn up."

Instead, Phish arrived to discover a full-scale festival going down, 70,000 people gathered for a bill which also featured Neil Young, Bonnie Raitt, David Crosby, Carole King, and Kenny Loggins. "I had no idea," Trey marveled. "They shuttled us onstage and there was this one mike. They said,

'Here's Phish!' All these people have never heard of us, and we're going, 'Here we go. What are we going to do?' That was pretty bad."

Looking as stunned as the audience felt, Phish performed two songs, unaccompanied renditions of "Amazing Grace" and "I Didn't Know," and, Trey grins, "I'm sure they thought we were pretty out there!" The significance of the day's date, and the proximity of so many superstars, did not go unnoticed, however. Midway through that evening's show, Phish took enormous pleasure in welcoming Neil Young onstage with them; then, as the audience roared its approval and shadowy figures shifted to the side of the stage, Fish returned to the microphone. "April Fool!"

The undoubted highlight of the spring tour was Phish's appearance at the two-day Laguna Seca Daze festival, in Monterey, California. High up a first-day bill which featured blind guitar wizard Jeff Healey, Shawn Colvin, Blues Traveler, and the headlining Allman Brothers, Phish turned in a performance which, *Relix* happily admitted, "delighted the audience. . . . Judging by the response they received, the crowd was really into the band's sonic whirlwind." Viewed from atop the Ferris wheel which dominated the rear of the raceway, Phish were little more than an indeterminate blob streaming into the afternoon sun. But they sounded sensational.

As was becoming their practice more and more, Phish scheduled a short break in their itinerary, dividing their tour into very distinct spring and summer segments.

They deserved the rest. Phish's July 1993 tour was to be their most extravagant yet, not in terms of dates, but in the nature of venues they would be hitting this time. Having reached a point where the only way to satisfy individual cities' ticket demands was to play either a lot of shows in smaller venues, or one or two in the larger halls, Phish went the whole hog and booked themselves into every East Coast amphitheater they could get.

Elsewhere, they returned to venues they had sold out just four months earlier, and set new speed records for ticket sales; elsewhere again, they jumped one, even two, rungs up the venue scale. The last time Phish had played Vancouver, B.C., in the spring, they headlined the 86th Street Music Hall. This time, they were packing the Commodore Ballroom. In both Seattle and Portland, they took over venues which were almost double the size they'd played back in April. What was most impressive, however, was the knowledge that next time out, they'd be moving even higher up the ladder.

At the same time, Phish's popularity remained surprisingly uneven. Just as they had on the spring tour, when a gold-plated run of sold-out theaters would suddenly be shattered by an all-but-empty-hall, ticket sales on the summer outing were fluctuating wildly. Having sold out two nights at the 3,000-capacity Tower in Upper Darby, Pennsylvania, in May, maybe Phish were overestimating their draw when they booked into the nearby Mann Music Center, with seating available to 13,000 Philadelphians. They attracted just 400 more bodies to that show than they'd just lured to the Tower; and, to make matters worse, as if such a thing were possible, two out of Phish's three lighting systems dropped dead where they stood. That left one, Chris Kuroda shudders, "which was not meant to light the band, it was meant to do a few other things, and that was all I had. Boy, that was just an awful night. It was huge, and I was just wigging, I was freaking out." At least there weren't too many witnesses.

The ticket torment continued. A massive 16,000 tickets went on sale for Phish's appearance at the Stowe Mountain Performing Arts Center in Vermont. Just 5,306 were sold, and, to add insult to that injury, the band were forced to curtail their open-air performance when the heavens opened up on them.

In Stanhope, New Jersey, less than 6,000 people turned up to rattle around the 12,000-capacity Waterloo Village, and there were less than 2,500 at the Meadow Brook Music festival in Rochester, Michigan—less than one-third of the venue's capacity.

Though it is easy to dwell on such figures, however, they were the exceptions. Theaters and auditoriums sold out almost as a matter of course. A colossal 15,000 fans attended the Great Woods Center in Mansfield, Massachusetts; 14,000 filled the Centrum in nearby Worcester, undaunted even by ticket prices which left little change out of $20, even $25.

Even more important, the fans who did attend the shows now describe the summer 1993 tour as one of the classic outings in Phish's entire history. Opening up to the vastness of the arenas confronting them, allowing both their music and their stage sets to swell to fill the void between stage and audience, Phish came of age in those enormous halls.

Trey reflects, "Sometimes you might have a large group of people and not play well, and then all you're thinking about is you didn't play well. Because . . . our success has been primarily live, it's meant that we'll grow slowly in certain areas by word of mouth. There will be more people in Boston than Miami, since we've played Boston something like fifteen times. But what's important to us is to feel like we're doing something progressive and new, and something we're happy with."

And they weren't too proud to eat humble pie when the occasion demanded. A show in Nashville, Tennessee, was so undersubscribed that, rather than set up on the huge, lonely stage, Phish played their set in the snack bar instead.

Although they were invited to attend many more, Phish

played just two shows on the 1993 H.O.R.D.E. tour, slipping them into their own schedule as time allowed, as the statisticians notched up another sure sign of their increasing personal draw. Neither did they contribute anything like their full-blown show to the proceedings. The sheer logistics of the show demanded that Phish curtail their performance to mere single-set appearances at the Orange County Fairgrounds in Middletown, New York, and the Classic Amphitheater in Richmond, Virginia, but so far as Trey was concerned, it would have been cruel to play any longer. "I thought the H.O.R.D.E. went a little long," he admitted later. "It was like eight hours, and I thought people would just get tired."

On August 28, 1993, Phish hit the University of California in Berkeley, for one of the strangest billings of their headlining career, an open-air theater packed to capacity not only for Phish, but also for the opener, J. J. Cale. It really was bizarre to see Cale, the Grand Old Man of laid-back blues rock, and probably the single most important influence on Eric Clapton's entire post-sixties output, coming onstage in bright sunshine. Smoky, mellow, and so-o-o laid-back, Cale was the kind of person who you imagined didn't even start breathing until the room was full of cigarette smoke and everyone was on to their second hair-of-the-dog. But here he was, in the raw afternoon, and only the shades (which he always wore anyway) suggested anything was out of the ordinary.

Every song, it seemed, was one you recognized, leaking out of a radio someplace, or leeching out from another Clapton album, but still Cale held the real favorites back until the end, the hebetudinous promise of "After Midnight," and the near-anthemic "Cocaine." Then, introducing Mike Gordon onstage to add bass to the big hits, Cale could have brought the house down if he'd only upped the pressure a bit.

As it was, the walls wavered a little, and everyone sang

along with "Cocaine," and really, they meant every word. The acid was very good that night, certainly better than plugging your nose up with ice and spending the rest of the night clearing phlegm from your throat. During the break, two Phish Heads were talking, touching politics with a gentle prod, then dismissing the subject with a snap of reality. "Who cares about Reagan, and homelessness and crap? If you really want to know why the 1980s sucked, don't look any further than the recreational drugs."

The show started strange, and kept getting stranger. The Dude of Life was at the show, making his first-ever appearance on a West Coast stage, and the vague mumblings around the theater reminded onlookers that though some people swore by the guy (and *Unbroken Chain* made some nice remarks, too), there were a lot of people who really couldn't stand the Dude, people who'd only read about him in the past, but who would happily see his omnipresent rubber chicken jammed uncomfortably someplace very dark. There were rumors that the Dude had an album on the way, the one he'd recorded with Phish back in 1991. He could probably stick that in the same place as the chicken.

Berkeley was a memorable show then, but for many people, especially the virtual army of fans who determined to trail Phish all the way for this tour, the summer's highlight had come a week before the Cale gig, when Phish crowned their conquest of Colorado, when they took over the legendary Red Rocks amphitheater for the first time.

There are a lot of people, of course, who insist that without U2, Red Rocks would be just another smartly lit amphitheater rising up among the dirty pink rocks that pepper the Colorado Rockies' foothills. And it's true, Red Rocks is not a unique phenomenon in the Rocky Mountain region, but it's an inspiring one all the same. A similar formation in Colorado

Springs was dubbed Garden of the Gods by the town's first settlers, and the name has stuck. So, but for very different reasons, has Red Rocks'.

Long a favorite haunt of traveling rock musicians, Red Rocks was selected as the venue for the single live performance which, more than any other in their career, can be said to have transformed U2 from a successful rock band into a very successful rock band. In 1983, the Irish quartet shot their first concert film there, for immediate broadcast on MTV, swiftly followed by a home video release and a live album, and even today, the memory of Bono outlined against the flaming heavens, a youthful mountain goat with a white flag for antlers, remains one of the ultimate icons of the 1980s.

It is only appropriate, then, that almost a full decade later, but on that same patch of stage, the rock-framed image of Mike and Trey, pogoing into the smoky air from their trusty trampolines, seems equally evocative of the decade which Phish have come to dominate.

WE WANTED TO DO IT EVERY NIGHT

December 1993 left the East Coast in the grip of the whitest winter since . . . since the last one, shivered the weather guy as the traffic crawled up I-95 out of Baltimore, and even when American University finally hove into view, there was no respite in sight.

A three-hour wait outside the arena, almost an hour once they let people inside, and most of the audience obviously felt equally miserable, because it was a grave in there, not a word, not a sound, just the incessant chatter of five thousand teeth and a volley of tubercular coughs which even made the medics edgy. And whose bright idea was it to physically pat down every person who entered, keeping everyone out in the cold even longer?

Bender Arena, in Washington, D.C., was Phish's first gig since the summer, their first since they completed work on their next album, *Hoist*, and the first of only four chances anyone would get to see them play before spring. "I bet they do 'It's Ice' tonight," someone hissed through frozen, cracking lips. "If they've got any sense, that's all they'll play," her partner responded through a mouthful of Chapstick.

The stage was the best thing to look at, a vast aquarium topped with swimming fish, bedecked in kelp and clams and shells. In the regular light, it looked unexcitingly dull, and in regular hands, it probably would have been. But this was Phish, this was a spectacle, and when the stage lights exploded, so did the stage, neon foam rubber giving the entire stage the look of an undersea paradise, or maybe a tropical fish tank.

Phish soundchecked with "Kashmir," the rolling Zeppelin classic which was one of the only reasons to buy the *Physical Grafitti* album, and expectations were high that they would play it again. Instead, the song turned up as a ghost riff in "Possum," and it was Zappa's "Peaches en Regalia" which kicked the show off, and "Highway to Hell" which wrapped it all up, two glorious sets of old and new. And of course they played "It's Ice," just to remind people what they could expect in the frozen hell that stretched away between D.C. and New Haven.

It was exactly a year since Phish had last played New Haven, a year during which their local standing soared from two nights at the picturesque Palace Theater, to one sold-out show at the Veterans' Memorial Coliseum. It was a neat-looking building, one of the few places with that name in the whole of America which actually looked like it meant it; how many old soldiers really want to be remembered by the concrete bunkers full of bleachers with which other cities saddle their heroes?

The Coliseum, though, was as civilized as the city, and as efficient as Father Christmas, who certainly seemed to be infecting the security. There was a genuine urge to get the lines moving quickly, and an almost solicitous ushering of frozen bodies into welcome warmth. Phish took the stage without delay or tardiness, and even the aquarium looked brighter tonight.

There was an extra-special buzz in the air, too. New Haven marked the first-ever appearance at a Phish gig of a special reserved seating area for tapers. It had been a long time since Paul Languedoc reluctantly decided to stop fans from patching in to his soundboard, exhausted and exasperated by the number of requests he received every night. Since then, taping was every man—and mike—for himself. Now, a whole section had been roped off, and the specially marked tickets, which guaranteed all those little sonic niceties which spelled the difference between a clean, sharp recording and a spool of magnetic soup, were snatched up within minutes. It was amazing to watch, too, as the fans filed in, how a few people who'd decided not to bring their equipment to the show after all, happily traded tickets with people who did. It was a far cry from the Dead shows, where a similar idea had long since been operating, where non-tapers deliberately bought up those highly prized tickets, then auctioned them off to the highest desperate bidder.

"Peaches en Regalia" remained in the set, prompting rumors already that Phish were planning a full-scale tribute to Zappa, who'd died at the beginning of the month. Aside from that, though, last night in D.C. was a fast retreating memory, as Phish unveiled what amounted to a greatest-hits set: "Foam" and "Glide," "Sparkle," "Stash," and not even a reprise of the almost raucous "Sample in a Jar" which previewed *Hoist* the night before. Indeed, there was nothing which they'd not played on the summer tour, but maybe that was the point. Tonight was a night of near–New Year's celebration, not the time to play with people's heads. Those surprises would be saved for the next night, in Portland, Maine.

The Cumberland County Civic Center is the regular home of the Portland Pirates, and you didn't have to know that to be aware that the venue served a purpose beyond major concerts. The Pirates' ice-rink playing field made its presence felt all night long, lying frozen beneath the floor, while everyone above it rubbed numb, freezing feet.

The snow locked in Maine like a Crusader with a chastity-belt key, and everywhere, knots of Phish Heads admitted that they'd been tempted to give this show a miss, just to be sure of reaching Worcester tomorrow. Everybody seemed to know at least one familiar face who went straight on, and afterward, those same people all said the same thing. If you missed out on Portland, you missed a real blinder.

"The amazing thing about Phish," says Saul Penman, "is the way they can take songs from their earliest days and still play them with freshness, enthusiasm, and zap." This night's performance of "David Bowie" was a case in point. The song was ten minutes long when it turned up on *Junta*, and they'd played it who knows how many times since (255, according to the *Pharmer's Almanac*). But it sounded brand-new when it turned up in the set; they treated it with love, and the respect it deserved, and the only change they might have to make wouldn't roll around until 1997, when the old boy wouldn't B40-something anymore.

"We do go through these cycles where we can't get enough of certain songs," Trey once remarked. "Like, we weren't playing 'Split Open and Melt.' And then halfway through the spring [1992] tour, we figured out a new way to play it, and then every night we wanted to do it.

"To me, it's more of the weight of the whole night . . . a 'What song is right for tonight?' A song is new for about half a tour, and then it's like everything else."

They dug into "Dream On," the Aerosmith anthem which the Mission resurrected so wonderfully almost a decade before, as if to prove a great song can be played in any style, so long as you don't lose its spirit. But the real killer was "Colonel Forbin's Ascent," which might be tried and truly trusted, but is also capable of transporting the audience as far as they want to go. "Surfin' U.S.A." in the middle of winter.

Considering they'd not played it more than a dozen times, Phish's a cappella "Free Bird" was another sight to behold, one of the most overdone songs in the entire rock 'n' roll repertoire transformed into a workout for some freakish barbershop quartet from hell. But had anyone else ever tried to re-create three lead guitar lines with nothing but their voices? And succeeded? As *Unbroken Chain* marveled, "They stand there, all four of them, and just WAIL it out, the song in its entirety, with their voices! I would, quite simply, pass out if it were me trying to do that."

The midshow break came much too quickly, but was over before most people even gathered their wits, an ominous *2001* looming out over the masses, blending with the fog that rolled in from the stage, deep, dark, disturbing, and even your neighbors were suddenly mere jolting shapes in the stroboscopic bath. "I Am Hydrogen" opened up into a sea of pure jamming, and when the fog started to clear, the trampolines were already out, Mike and Trey leaping higher and higher. If this had been the last night of the tour, the last night of the year, the world could have ended with the biggest bang it could manage, and no one would have noticed.

Except for the people who'd bought tickets for the real New Year's Eve show—poor, unsuspecting lambs that they were.

Few people at a Phish concert have ever experienced life in a police state. Being a teenage concertgoer in Seattle comes close, with the city's teen dance ordinances and a minimal lifespan for all-ages clubs—and trying to buy beer on a Sunday in Boston isn't easy, either. But genuine jackbooted, truncheon-wielding fascists are not a common sight in America, unless, of course, you're frozen to the bone and hallucinating hellishly while you try to negotiate security at the Centrum in Worcester, Massachusetts, in the midst of the city's own First Night festivities. The fact that the Centrum itself is painted a gaudy dirty orange only added to the surrealism. Imagine the Nuremberg rallies in an underfunded fruit bowl.

IDs were flashed, and then flashed again. A Good Conduct certificate notarized by three dead presidents might have got you in hassle-free, but what the security teams really wanted, it seemed, was for everybody to simply surrender their tickets, then make their way quietly home without delay. On the other side of the coin, of course, you could understand the hireling goons' twitchy nervousness. Would you let someone dressed as a cow into a concert?

The neon shark swam in unmolested, but the cow was frisked, and so was the llama, and people were still coming into the auditorium ten, fifteen minutes into the show, asking what they'd missed, and cursing the cops who'd made the whole night such a hassle. Then a stage-diver simply dropped from the heavens, and found a soft landing on so many unprepared shoulders.

Onstage, Phish were in full bloom. A vaguely Hawaiian-looking Tom Marshall appeared, looking like he'd just stepped out of the shower. Perpetually stage-shy, Phish's favorite lyricist sang a few lines of "Run Like an Antelope," and then did precisely that. He was offstage before some people even knew they'd seen him.

There was an unmistakable air of celebration building, as the first set ended and the second one started with a magnificent "Tweezer." And with ten minutes till midnight, and "You Enjoy Myself" in full, frenzied flight, the climax was so close you could taste it. Still playing their instruments, but winding down the song, the group members began pulling on rubber suits, wet suits like skin divers, and flapping around in snorkels and flippers.

"We'll see you in fifteen," waved Trey, and while the crowd simply bellowed, the speakers roared out the sound of the sea. "We're going on a little excursion," Trey added, and one half expected a yellow submarine to emerge. Instead, more skin divers, maybe Phish, maybe not, could be heard above the stage, talking about diving, and how they hated their wet suits.

Slowly they lowered themselves into the fish tank, cords around their midsections as they sank into the "sea," down toward the giant clamshell where they normally stowed the stage props. It opened and they disappeared. "It's like Spinal Tap on acid," roared someone, but it was more like Esther Williams straight.

Phish were up to something. The figures vanished, and the tape was dying down, but the clam was rising up, opening its mouth, and beginning the countdown: Ten . . . nine . . . eight . . . three . . . two . . . one—Happy 1994!—and Phish blew back out, into "Auld Lang Syne," while white balloons ricocheted around the seething crowd, and old acquaintances introduced a new friend, "Down with Disease," a song from the next album which they'd never played live before.

"Suzie Greenberg" was next, amply infused with some Zappa-esque twists, while an Uncle Frank look-alike glided his way across the stage. Neil Diamond's "Cracklin' Rosie," a manic "Harry Hood," and then back into "Down with Disease" to prove that the new songs might be shorter, but they offered room to maneuver regardless.

The third set ended where the second one began, with "Tweezer Reprise," then back for "Golgi Apparatus" and good-bye with "Amazing Grace." The crowd kept on singing until the goons took out the cattle prods.

Phish's fifth album, *Hoist*, was scheduled for a March 29, 1994, release, and it was a mark of the band's shift in perspective that of the eleven tracks included on the disc, only four—"Sample in a Jar," "Axcilla," "Lifeboy," and most recently, "Down with Disease"—had ever been played live. (A fifth, "Buffalo Bill," made one in-concert appearance, but would be dropped from the album before its release.)

That scenario, of course, would change once Phish returned to the road in the spring, with a semisecret hometown show on April 4, before the outing proper kicked off the following day in Montreal. Until then, however, the Phish Net buzzed with rumor and speculation, with a correspondent to America Online's Grateful Dead forum adding to the hubbub with an early preview of the album. "If you are familiar with the [Rolling Stones'] *Sticky Fingers, Exile on Main Street,* or [Eric Clapton's] *Slowhand,* then you'll have some idea of the overall feel of the piece—warm like a fireplace, very live and very vibrant."

"It's actually my favorite [of all our albums]," Mike pledged later. "It's more easily fun to listen to, not as heavy and lengthy, and it was probably the most fun to record, too. I sort of hear that when I play it back. It's the one album where, even after a few weeks of making it, and listening to each song eight hundred times, I felt like I could put it in my car and it still felt good to hear."

Looking back a couple of years later, Mike was able to put the album, and the attendant live shows, in better perspective. "It was the time, he admitted to *High Times,* "when everything was very fast. But the problem gets to be not just tempo. Something else changes that is more subtle. It's which part of the beat we are playing on, whether we are playing ahead of the beat or behind the beat. It's more enjoyable if it's behind the beat." Too much of *Hoist,* it would transpire, was ahead of the beat; too much of it, for want of a better expression, rocked out.

Prompted by their A&R person, Nancy Jeffries, who was

adamant that the band should try and make an album that didn't sound like it ought to be live, Phish complied with another change in producer. Out went Barry Beckett, in came Paul Fox, a studio magician whose track record was as firmly rooted in the "alternative" world as Beckett's was in the classics. The Sugarcubes (Björk's Icelandic aggregation), Gene Loves Jezebel, and 10,000 Maniacs numbered among Fox's past accomplishments (more recently, he worked with Seattle space-rockers Sky Cries Mary), and though none of them could exactly be said to have impacted upon Phish's own musical topography, the producer's experience was to have a profound effect on the group all the same.

It was Fox, for instance, who suggested Fish try using a different snare drum on every track, to ensure a different sound each time; Fox, too, who proposed that Phish break away from New England and try recording for once in Los Angeles, at Woodland Hills' American Recording Company. Both turned out to be winning ideas; it would be another two years before Fish finally gave up the snare-drum idea, while the complete change in scenery meant that the band would not be distracted. "We were not near our homes," Mike explained, "so we were focused on the project like never before."

In fact, they were so focused that not only did they happily adopt another record-company suggestion—that they try once more to write some radio-friendly songs—they also renounced their original idea of giving the album the distinctly juvenile, if humorously penile, title of *Hung Like a Horse*—which of course would have undone every other friendly move they made. Instead, Phish simply insinuated the suggestion, co-opting one of Amy Skelton's horses, Maggie, and hanging her up for the front-cover shot.

Phish's refusal to air great swaths of *Hoist* before entering the studio, meanwhile, was a deliberate attempt to fashion an album which would grow into the live environment, rather than vice versa. Of course, they had tried to do that before, most volubly with the last of their independent releases, *Lawn Boy*. But they were working on their own then, and largely for their own satisfaction. Now, other factors came into play, not least of all the need to prove to Elektra that the label was right to pick up its option for the next brace of Phish albums. And that, in turn, meant Paul Fox would be called upon not only to establish the mood and sound of the record, but would contribute to the arrangements, too—a situation which was utterly new for Phish.

In September 1993, Phish and Fox met for the first pre-production sessions, where the shape of the eventual album would be sketched out. The meeting was even more productive than they expected.

"For the first time," Mike marveled, "we actually wrote and arranged songs for an album." He told *Relix*, "It was not like we came to Paul with ten-minute songs and said, 'Help us cram these down,' as we had done before with other albums. The songs were made to be uplifting, accessible, fun and concise."

Trey agreed. "Making records is a different experience from playing live. For a while, people said that our records sounded like a live band that stopped by a studio and decided to play a couple of tunes, which is basically what they were. They sounded real flat. We would write these songs, go out for a tour and play the songs, and the songs would develop in front of a live audience. [But] when you get into the studio and you try to play the song, it's not going to be the same. There's nothing you can do about it." And later, he would continue enthusing, "What surprised people is that our songs came out a lot more straightforward and simple. Now that we're playing them live, they're stretching out, and I feel a certain excitement there. Plus the songs are a lot more songy."

"We met [Paul] and we clicked with him right away," Mike remarked, and from that empathy there developed the trust Phish needed to establish before they would let Fox do their arrangements; a trust, they now revealed, which they did not extend to Barry Beckett. "Paul was really good at conducting the recording sessions and keeping them mellow and moving them along," Mike continues. "If we did a few takes of a song, and he knew that after a few takes it's not gonna happen, he would push us along to something else and say, 'I think we better come in tomorrow.' He had a good sensibility to him."

On the other hand, Trey revealed that a couple of the songs which made it onto the album were actually first takes, which simply couldn't be improved upon. "We worked out an arrangement of 'If I Could' and we hadn't quite gotten it. We set up the mikes and it was almost there. Then we got it and it was the first time we ever really played the song. What I learned from that is, the creation of the song has an energy to it. Then when you bring it out live, you get a whole new kind of excitement, but it's hard to go back."

Fox also encouraged Phish to broaden their sound: Mike reckons he "probably used five different basses" on the album; Jon, six different snare drums. The renowned Tower of Power horn section was recruited to lend their weight to "Julius" and "Wolfman's Brother"; Bela Fleck brought his banjo along to the sessions; and Sly Stone's wife, Rosie, sang on "Down with Disease." There was even a guest-vocals appearance from singer-songwriter Alison Krauss. Krauss, says Mike, was "someone who we just met in a bar that she was singing and playing at. It was really lucky because we've always loved her singing. We walked up after her gig and said, 'Will you play on our album?' and she agreed to."

Although its predecessors enjoyed their fair share of reviews, *Hoist* would become the first Phish album to be afforded truly major press attention. Moving away from the cozy confines of the "alternative to alternative" market which had nurtured them for so long, Phish were now thrust into the heart of the mainstream beast. Inevitably, the results were not always pleasing.

A write-up in *Entertainment Weekly* set the stage for future detractors with its references to "kooky lyrics, musical flashiness and boogie-fied tunes . . . some ungodly hybrid of Frank Zappa and the Marshall Tucker Band." And then it came down even harder. "The truly wonderful thing about Phish is the way they make you appreciate other bands, like, oh, Mudhoney," wrote reviewer Tom Sinclair. "If punk had never happened, you can bet more rock records would suffer from this sort of overly eclectic pretentiousness."

In his eyes, it seemed, *Hoist* was all but unsellable. It was deeply ironic, then, that to many of Phish's fans, it was nothing short of a sellout. Even a generally complimentary review in *Relix* could not resist remarking, "It's the band's most produced and commercial effort to date," and then warned fans, "Don't let that deter you," as though the writer knew that it would. Those fears and feelings would catalyze around the news that Phish were filming a video for "Down with Disease."

As a band, Mike insisted, Phish discussed the possibility of making a video "for years beforehand"; even more pertinently, when the band's A&R person, Nancy Jeffries, first mooted the idea a year before, during the *Rift* sessions, Mike was ready to start the cameras rolling there and then.

On that occasion, he was shouted down by his bandmates, and Trey was forthright about the reasons for Phish's recalcitrant stance. "MTV is fucking up music," he told *High Times*. "It's very sad that people start to think of the video before they think about the song. The beauty of music is that you can create images in your mind while listening." It was an old, old argument, but it was one in which Phish fervently believed.

A year later, however, Jeffries returned to the fray, and this time her ideas were more compelling than ever before. So was Mike's support for them, particularly when he was offered the director's chair. Not only would he be supervising the video, he pledged, he would also be able to use it against that crack squad of Phish Head assassins who delighted in transforming the "Letters" page of the *Doniac Schvice* newsletter into a virtual battleground of ethics and morality.

"Fans are often upset about changes, and since we're all about change, it's sort of a silly thing to be upset about," Mike swore disdainfully. "Trying different mediums is just one thing that we do at times. It just seemed the right time for a video. It's not like we're going to start doing Coke commercials."

Remarks like that surely missed the point of the protests, though. For many people, the problem with Phish making a video had nothing to do with the group selling out, or even with the possibility of a big hit bringing more people into the scene. Certainly some fans felt that way, but the real resistance came from people who believed Phish stood for something purer than other groups.

There's an established order to the music business today, a routine which developed in the 1980s, and essentially demands a band follow a set route with every release. Making videos, of course, was an integral part of that route.

Up to this point, Phish steadfastly avoided falling into that trap. For other groups, gaps of eighteen months, even two years, were now customary between new albums. Phish, however, stuck to the album-a-year approach which was the norm back when they were kids, first buying albums. Other bands toured once for each record. Phish often hit the same cities two or three times a year, remaining on the road for twice as long as they were off it. And other groups made videos. With that line of defense now breached, what was next? Would Phish become just "another" band as well?

The "Down with Disease" video was a relatively straightforward affair, revolving around a merry sequence of scuba-diving in a fish tank, cut with scenes from the New Year's Eve show. It was entertaining, but very contrived, and many Phish Heads simply passed it by in despair.

The diving scenes, however, would at least win the Beavis and Butt-head seal of utter bemusement.

Butt-head began the exchange. "Cool. They're, like, diving into the fish tank."

"The what?"

"The fish tank."

"Oh. I thought those things were just fancy clear toilets."

"Beavis, you think everything's a toilet."

"Well, there's a fish in there. And they go to the bathroom, right? So it's a toilet."

Nor were America's favorite delinquents alone in their puzzlement. Trey and Page shared it as well, although for entirely different reasons. Responding as much to the fact that the video made no difference whatsoever to the group's commercial standing, as to Phish's fans' undisguised hostility, Trey described "Down with Disease" as "a momentary lapse of reason." He insisted Phish neither wanted to do it nor—director Mike notwithstanding—enjoyed making it. People can tell when a band is betraying itself, he affirmed. "They listen and they can hear the intent."

And yet, as crimes against humanity go, "Down with Disease" was scarcely in the ballpark when compared with some outfits' video attempts, and it was all the more ironic that within weeks of "Down with Disease" hitting the circuit, Phish released a second video through their own mail-order service, which made "Down with Disease" look like the height of both art and integrity.

Tracking was hyped as a behind-the-scenes look at the making of *Hoist*, shot by Mike, and comprised of random cuts of conversation, barely audible rehearsals, and sing-alongs . . . and if that sounds unimpressive, it was. *Tracking* was bad, it was banal, but most damaging of all, it was boring, and the wonder is that with all the flak descending upon "Down with Disease," from which Phish received no direct profit, few people spoke out against *Tracking*.

Or maybe there is nothing to wonder about whatsoever, and Mike's belief that the fans were simply afraid of change is borne out after all. *Tracking* was made for the existing fans, who could take their own chances on the merits of the piece. "Down with Disease" was aimed at attracting new fans, and the way concert tickets were being snapped up these days, the last thing Phish needed was fresh competition from the MTV crowd.

Whatever the reasons, the "Down with Disease" video remains a low point in Phish's own self-esteem, and one for which they would still be apologizing a year or more later. "As one tries to establish oneself in this industry, it's easy to get influenced," Page apologized. "Different people want you to do different things. It's a business to most people.

"There was a time"—and this was it—"when we were not as pure or as true as we could have been, which is a natural phenomenon. In the push and pull, you're bound to bend a little. But we've started to take everything back. It's our career." From here on in, he was adamant, "We're only going to do what makes us happy." Trey concurred. "We barely talk to anybody at the record company anymore. They've essentially given up. And thank God for that."

Mike, a little more generously, and certainly less idealistically, continued, "The record company . . . haven't pushed us toward those kinds of goals more than we've been wanting to go." But he acknowledged that in the disastrous wake of "Down with Disease," "More than ever, they want to let us do our own thing. They want to sell records, but I think that they're letting us be what we are. They've kind of accepted that we're probably not gonna be a Top-40 band."

On March 29, 1994, *Hoist* entered the *Billboard* chart at number 34.

THE PAPER CUT ACROSS THE NIPPLE

For a group to vault from bar-band status to the American stadium circuit in under five years is not unusual. Indeed, in the mid-1990s' days of instant superstardom, it might even be considered a little tardy. Acts like Hootie and the Blowfish, Bush, and the Black Crowes, after all, made a similar leap almost literally overnight, while Joan Osborne made the transition from second stage at H.O.R.D.E. to number one on the charts with equal haste.

But to an audience who grew on its own exclusivity, who reveled in the knowledge that for many people out there, Fish was still the ex-singer with eighties prog-rockers Marillion, it was a major shock, and an unpleasant one at that, to suddenly find swaths of the quartet's spring 1994 tour moving into stadium-sized venues.

Mike told *Relix*, "Making the transition from smaller to larger venues has been gradual for us, and I think that's healthier in a way, than bands who have these hit songs and are playing huge places [immediately]. It takes practice to perform in bigger halls, there can be such vastness."

Phish viewed the switch with some distaste, of course,

dreading the perceived loss of intimacy which was so vital to their initial growth. But by midway through Phish's spring 1994 tour, Mike was adamant. "We love playing in bigger places now. It's exciting. It's true we can't see the people in the back rows as well; before, we could maybe make eye contact with a high percentage of the house. [But] we love the acoustics in the big rooms, and sometimes the vibe is just as good, sometimes better than a small room. . . . Also, it lets us communicate more and listen to each other more, and that's what it's all about anyway."

He told *Gallery of Sound Gazette*, "There are some nice things about intimate groups, but huge groups can seem intimate, too. More of a challenge in some ways, but it's a challenge to loosen up and be ourselves. I mean, I guess when you reach twenty thousand–something, it's hard to feel intimate with the people up on the lawn and the back rows. And that, I guess, is a shame. But for me, it depends on other things so much more than the size of the venue. Like the acoustics, or whether I've been practicing, or whether I feel comfortable, or if my mental state is pleasant. Those kinds of things really add up to more for me.

"When we first started playing in larger places, even the first time we played in a theater, I felt more self-conscious not being immersed in people, because they were either far away or on the other side of the orchestra pit, and that sort of thing. I overcame that. [But] those kinds of attitude things are . . . important. People seem happy. I mean, there are a lot of people that complain that we're playing the larger venue, but the crowds grew. Also, it makes it so that we can have a bigger production and some more of the things we want. Like, if we were still playing in clubs, we probably couldn't carry a grand piano. I like the sound of that better than the synthesized version."

He also reminded fans that Phish's new status was the

result of continuous growth and not, as in the case of so many other groups, a sudden development. "Even on this tour, we're just doing a couple of arenas, and we had already done arenas playing with other bands, like the H.O.R.D.E., or the Santana thing. So it's like we got our foot in the door, we got used to it, seeing all those people."

That was true. But truth didn't compensate the legions of loyal supporters who followed the group through thick, thin, and thinner, and who were now being locked out of the party. For that situation to be remedied, the band would need to take yet another page out of the Grateful Dead's book and establish their own fans-only ticket hotline. And until that could finally be put into effect, it was every fan for himself, an attitude which of course bred even greater distress.

Too many bands forgot their roots as they made the inevitable ascent up the ladder; too many, like Spin Doctors, watched their original core following simply fade away, overwhelmed by the struggle to reconcile its love for the group with that of two million merry mainstream purchasers of *A Pocketful of Kryptonite*. The famous lone voice screaming, "Remember Nectar's?" at Phish's summer 1993 show in Stowe, Vermont, was merely one of many firstborn Phish Heads who could no longer justify their devotion, and in the parking lot outside Seattle's Moore Theater—a veritable dwarf compared with some of the East Coast venues Phish was hitting—there was a sadder sight yet.

"I saw Phish the first time they played these parts," Bill lamented to anyone who approached him, "at Southern Oregon State, in 1991." He admitted he was a latecomer, compared to some of the long-term converted he knew, but what he lacked in road miles, he'd made up in tapes. There must have been three hundred tapes in the boxes behind him, piled up in the back of his pickup truck, and just as many people converging on him, drawn by the sign which read, Live

Phish Tapes, Free. The only problem, for potential pickers at least, was the nature of the tapes. Bill's entire collection was preserved on 8-tracks.

They sounded much better than cassettes, he insisted; the tape is wider and it moves a lot slower, so more information can be stored. He'd made custom labels, hand-lettered and-drawn, and a few of the tapes he'd recorded himself, hauling a big old battered recorder to shows, ignoring the puzzled looks of the digital kids around him. It really was a labor of love, but now the romance was over.

Bill continued his lament. "Seventeen-fifty for the ticket itself, booking fees, parking-lot charges—the entire concert industry has been hijacked by highwaymen, and I'm just better off out of it." And while no one knows how many of the Phish Heads pawing through his collection actually owned the equipment to play those tapes on, the joyous cries of, "You've got this show, man," "What a score," and "I've found it," suggested there'd be a lot of people buying the stuff in the future.

Phish's spring 1994 tour opened at the Flynn Theater in Burlington, a show which debuted much of the newly released *Hoist*, reintroduced the Giant Country Horns for one night only, and raised money to help with the planned renovation of the old theater.

Packed to the rafters though it was, the Flynn was the smallest venue Phish would visit this time around, and the band clearly gloried in this last taste of genuine intimacy. Indeed, they swiftly received a somewhat backhanded, but nevertheless laudatory, compliment when a high-quality recording of the show, *Phishin' at the Flynn*, appeared on the CD bootleg market, one of the first Phish boots to be so widely circulated.

Since that time, of course, Phish have become a definite favorite on the bootleg market, an unavoidable consequence of the ready availability of live tapes, but also a gauge not only of the band's commercial success, but of their collectibility, too.

A spokesman for one of Europe's most visible bootleg labels, the San Marino, Italy–based Kiss the Stone, believes that "Phish, like many other bands, have realized how important it is to have not only a live following, but also a certain amount of live product on the street, which counts as extra promotion for the band [and] in turn generates an interest in them as a live band. Although there are many live tapes to be found, most people still prefer to have a good CD copy." Two Kiss the Stone titles, *Follow Me to Gamehendge*, from 1992, and 1994's *Simple*, bear him out. Both rate amongst KTS's best-selling releases of all time.

Over at Elektra, of course, opinions differed considerably from these. There was outrage, for instance, that the music could be released for other people's profit, and concern that normal standards of quality control (*Tracking* presumably notwithstanding) could be compromised by factors out of the company's own reach. The very fears Elektra expressed when they first signed Phish, that widespread taping would inevitably lead to widespread bootlegging, were now being justified with a vengeance, and, to make matters worse, there was very little that could be done about it.

Thanks to differing copyright laws across Europe and Asia, the vast majority of CD bootlegs remain completely legal in their country of manufacture, while a late-1996 poll conducted by Kiss the Stone indicated that a very large number of American music buyers actively supported their activities. Any band publicly allying itself with the major labels' own profit-driven drive to eliminate bootlegging also stood a very good chance of alienating the very people it relied on to buy their official releases.

And so *Phishin' at the Flynn* was followed by a horde of

other titles, so many that in November 1996, the bootleg magazine *Live! Music Review* was forced to expand its own long-running survey of Grateful Dead releases, "Deadlines," to incorporate the deluge of new Phish titles ("Phish Tales"). Four Phish bootlegs were reviewed in the first column alone. The following month, Phish dominated the entire page.

The group's own contributions to this debate have been interesting. According to Kiss the Stone's spokesman, "A band that lets a live recording take place can be looked upon from two different directions. Either they believe that if they flood the market with live material, the bootleg industry will find it harder to sell their product, which is not true. Or, they believe their fans have the right to record their live performance, even if it does end up being released as a bootleg. I think that Phish, like the Grateful Dead, fall into the second category."

That would certainly appear to be the case. Tacitly acknowledging that if they could not beat the bootleggers, they could at least ensure that their fans did not suffer from poor-quality releases, Phish began downloading their own soundboard recordings onto the Phish Net. Several excellent bootlegs have emerged from this source.

In May 1994, however, a concert recording went into distribution which not only caused a serious rift in Phish's ranks, it ultimately led to the entire operation going into hiatus. To this day, Phish themselves have maintained a stoic silence over the details of their decision, and tapers continue to argue over what went wrong. What is certain, however, is that one unnamed group member, unhappy with some aspect of the performance, went ballistic when recordings from the Dallas Bomb Factory were downloaded into officially sanctioned circulation, and at least one *Pharmer's Almanac* reviewer, Katie Silver, acknowledges that she herself has reservations about the recording.

"I don't really, really, enjoy listening to this. It's interesting, sure, but it doesn't hold together . . . the way the ones from Bangor or Bozeman do." Was it this suggestion of unscheduled looseness which scarred the performance in the eyes of the unidentified Phish? Or is there something even more objectionable lurking within the mix someplace?

A disaster of a completely different nature befell Phish elsewhere on the tour. Soundchecking one evening, Trey fell into what Mike insists was "a hole in the stage," and broke his ankle. The show, of course, would go on, but the superstitious Trey was to remain cautious throughout the remainder of the outing, and not only for the sake of his foot.

Mike sniggers, "We had a song, 'I'm in a Hole,' which is a stupid song that we probably played twice, and then Trey fell in a hole and broke his ankle." Now, he continued, the guitarist was wandering around wondering which Phish lyric was going to come to pass next, and suffering pains of certainty that he knew what it was. One of Trey's greatest—if most unlikely—fears, Mike revealed, was that he would somehow, someday, have one of his nipples sliced, a horror which he incorporated into not one song but two: "The Sloth" and "Fee." " 'The paper cut across the nipple,' " Mike grinned. "He's thinking that the nipple slicing is going to come true."

In the meantime, Trey's injury necessitated some revision to Phish's live performance, not least of all the trampolining finale. In Lexington, Dave Matthews, leader of the eponymous opening act, was co-opted to replace him, with the remainder of the Dave Matthews Band then joining him onstage for a vacuum cleaner–led jam which only slowly metamorphosed into a beautiful version of "Somewhere Over the Rainbow." "The further out we take our music," Page mused afterward, "the more our fans seem to like it."

Idly he speculated, "We provide an emotional and spiritual experience for the audience," although as the tour progressed, one did wonder precisely how spiritual the sight of opera singer Andrea Baker was, singing a Puccini aria while Phish hurled boxes of mac-and-cheese into the Warfield Theater stalls; or how emotional a chorus of "Run, O. J., Run!" might be, as performed that famous evening when the accused football star fled down the expressway, with the full weight of the LAPD hot in pursuit behind him. Clearly, Phish's appeal also contained a fair degree of conspiratorial glee as well!

The tour introduced Phish into venues they might never have dreamed of playing. To much of their audience, however, it was very much a magical history tour, as *Unbroken Chain* editor Laura Paul Smith remarked to her readers. "The extended tour . . . has taken them to a number of fine theaters and venues us [Dead]heads might not get the opportunity to see a show at otherwise. Places like the Beacon Theater in New York, the 'Fabulous' Fox Theater in Atlanta, the Capitol Theater in Passaic, New Jersey, and the Tower Theater in Philadelphia, Red Rocks, and the Greek Theater in Berkeley are just a few of the places Phish has played. If you look at [the Dead's own facts and statistics guide] Deadbase, say around 1976, you'll see a number of theaters listed where Phish are currently making the rounds."

Phish would also be visiting several places where the Dead would never play again, venues which slapped outright bans on the band, usually after complaints about drug abuse. On July 10, 1994, Phish played the Saratoga Performing Arts Center, in Saratoga Springs, one of the most vociferously Dead-free zones in America; they had already lured hordes of Deadheads back to the University of Oregon in Eugene, and Merriweather Post Pavilion in Columbia, Maryland—other venues whose portals were hitherto regarded as Dead-proof.

Unfortunately, the Phish crowd could not necessarily be guaranteed to behave any better than their castigated contemporaries. "Spillover bad habits from Dead tours have [already] become a part of this scene," wrote *Unbroken Chain*'s Rebecca Quate, and those journalists and observers who chose to, found her complaints vividly illustrated by the experiences not only of fans, ripped off by so-called "brothers," but elsewhere, too.

Cary D. had been trading tapes for years before he moved into selling CD bootlegs of the bands he followed: the Allmans, the Dead, and most recently, Phish. "A lot of fans generally hold no bias toward CD bootlegs," he explained; "some even prefer them, particularly those who found that tape trading tends to put severe limitations on available time if you already have a busy work schedule and family responsibilities—a life."

It was a short-lived venture. Selling his stock from his van, on the way to shows or in the parking lot afterward, he now curses, "If you took a poll among bootleg dealers, and I talked to a lot of them, you will find that Phish and Grateful Dead fans are among the most active in both *buying* and *stealing* bootlegs. Somehow, some of the 'faithful' have come to the conclusion that since the bands condone free trades of tapes, and say the performances are meant to be freely distributed among fans, it is justifiable to liberate a CD dealer from his merchandise."

Several hundred dollars' worth of stolen stock was all it took to send Cary back to the less-tempestuous waters of tape trading, but he remains puzzled by the thieves' logic. "There was no trade. The obligation in a tape trade would have been to return a different performance desired by the trading partner. The 'liberator' of the CD has not met his/her obligation for an exchange."

Nor was petty thievery the only bad habit which Phish Heads seemed to have inherited. Suddenly, the hallucinogenic drug culture which the Dead are almost single-handedly blamed for dragging into the 1980s and 1990s, was exploding out of the Phish underground at such a rate that one was almost reminded of Pete Townshend's infamous condemnation of the original Woodstock festival: "Even the mud was spiked with acid!" Except acid was no longer the number one drug of choice. Now it was nitrous oxide.

Popularly, if a little self-disparagingly, referred to as hippie crack, nitrous is underground entrepreneuring at its creative best. And it was only sadly inevitable that it could be traced back to the Deadhead community. By the early 1990s, policing of their gatherings attained such peaks that simply contemplating the purchase of "regular" drugs seemed to carry a mandatory five-to-ten, and if anybody doubted that, they needed only examine the pitiful roll call of Heads Behind Bars which *Relix* contemplated with ever-increasing regularity.

Laughing gas, however, was legal in many states. Nitrous itself is readily available as a propellant in cans of whipped cream and cake frosting, while few childhood visits to the dentist were ever complete without a few lungfuls to lull the patient into slumber. Jacked into a colorful balloon—one more joyful accoutrement at a gig that's already a party—who could ever suspect what was really going on?

The gas was also cheap; a twenty-pound tank of the gas cost around $55, sufficient to fill several hundred of the balloons, and *High Times*, the monthly journal of the recreational drug user, had long since condemned the hordes of "genuine mobsters attracted by the 1,000 percent profit margin on laughing gas" who followed the cash scent to the crowds outside Phish shows. Five bucks a shot, and you can reuse the balloon afterward.

You would want to, as well. Nitrous has a notoriously powerful but frustratingly brief high, just a couple of minutes of total incapacity. Unfortunately, what is great for the dealers' return business has also been linked to some particularly nasty side effects. Scientific tests insist that prolonged abuse can eventually cause damage to the user's cerebral cortex, reproductive system, and bone marrow. Throw temporary addiction, long-term memory loss, delirium, and death into the sea of possibilities, and the slow tide of states which are now legislating against N20—a drug which medical insiders have been happily getting smashed on ever since it was discovered over two hundred years ago—has some sound grounds for continuing.

For most users, of course, the most immediate side effect is no worse than falling flat on your face after taking a hit. The old adage about simultaneously chewing gum and walking is one that nitrous freaks have long since learned not to laugh at, but still it was easy to find the nearest dealer, even without the balloons floating high to tip you off. You just followed the trail of suddenly incapacitated hippies.

Not that dealers made any serious attempt to hide their wares; and Mike, fully cognizant of the problem, acknowledged Phish's disgust. "If we're known as the nitrous band, we won't be able to play anywhere." Parking lots around Phish shows suddenly seemed to be littered with tanks, and for the cops policing the crowd, well aware of what was going on, it was a nightmare. Even those dealers busted for reckless endangerment, often the most powerful weapon in the legal arsenal, could plead total ignorance: "Hey officer, I'm just selling pretty balloons. It's not my fault if people want to empty them into their lungs, again . . . and again . . . and again."

Nor was it their fault that sometimes a couple of headfuls of gas was the only way one could actually make it through the night. Atlanta, on April 23, 1994, was a case in point. A masterstroke of truly malicious fate decreed that the Phish show at the Fox should coincide with the city's Freaknik festival, a gathering of Afro-American college students from all over the country. That, in turn, coincided with a gig by the rapper of the moment, Snoop Doggy Dogg; and just to add some flavor to the pot, the Atlanta Braves were playing a home game as well. Could an already hot city get any hotter?

Not according to the hundreds of Phish Heads who, gridlocked amid the Freaknik revelers, or caught in the game crowd without a traffic cop in sight, missed great chunks of the first set, sometimes hunks of the second, as they fought through a city under siege . . . and that despite the gig itself beginning forty-five minutes late. Inside, it was Phish business as usual; outside, though, people were still coming in as the crowd was filing out, and, as if to add a little more despair to the latecomers' day, it was only the following morning that they discovered the party had carried on after-hours, elsewhere. Partying at the Variety Playhouse in Little Five Points, Phish joined Merl Saunders and the Rainforest Band for an exquisite early-morning jam.

Nevertheless, there were plenty more opportunities to see Phish share out their stage as the tour wound on: at the SunFest festival in West Palm Beach, where Blues Traveler were just one of the day's other attractions; in Antioch, Tennessee, where Alison Krauss leaped up to sing "If I Could"; in Saratoga Springs, where the Dude of Life reappeared; and, just to keep everything in the family, at Penn State University, where the ubiquitous Mimi Fishman emerged to play cymbals on "I Didn't Know."

There was also the night in Columbia, South Carolina, when Page's father joined Phish onstage for encore performances of "Bill Bailey" and the aptly named "Father/Son Boogie." "To be invited by your son to join in the limelight is an unspeakable joy," Dr. McConnell admitted afterward. He could have looked totally out of place, a walking incongruity, as he took the stage with Phish, but he didn't. Neither did he show any signs of stage fright, even with a near-capacity

9,000-plus crowd baying in front of him. "I get misty-eyed just thinking about it."

The spring tour ended with the now-traditional Laguna Seca Daze festival in Monterey. Less than two weeks later, Phish's summer tour got under way, as the band ventured away from the coasts; away, on a few notable occasions, from civilization itself. Trey himself dubbed this leg of the outing the "You Snooze, You Lose" tour, as Phish hit venues far from the customary rock 'n' roll pathway, then treated the hardy faithful to some of the most adventurous sets of the year. And none so much as the Charleston Municipal Auditorium gig, when Gamehendge was revisited for only the fourth time, before Phish launched into an equally complete recounting of the *Hoist* album. Gamehendge, surprisingly, reappeared just two weeks later, at Great Woods in Mansfield, Massachusetts; less surprising now, was the news that Phish were looking seriously into the possibility of producing a CD-ROM of the entire saga. In the meantime, however, there was a new conventional album to think about. Recording began with the first show of the summer tour.

The news that Phish's next album would be the live document which the fans had been demanding for so long seemed to reinvigorate band and audience alike. Tapes from this tour offer up some of Phish's finest all-around performances, while not even the most careful live taper could avoid capturing some sense of the crowd's wild enthusiasm. But if anybody thought that with the live album Phish's promise had at last attained its peak, they would have another think coming.

As Halloween 1994, Phish's eleventh anniversary, approached, the idea began to flourish that it would be nice to do something particularly special. Widespread Panic had already institutionalized the date as one on which anything could happen, and Phish, too, had tried in the past to make it a little out of the ordinary. This year, however, would skew even further out, a one-off performance which only the lucky few at Phish's Glens Falls birthday party would witness. Phish already played all their own albums to death—wouldn't it be great to go out and play someone else's?

The individual group members drew up their own lists of possibilities, of albums they felt they could learn in the little time that would be available. Then they circulated the list through the *Doniac Schvice* newsletter. They already knew what they could do; it was left to the fans to decide the fine details.

Frank Zappa's *Joe's Garage*, Led Zeppelin's *Physical Graffiti*, Pink Floyd's *Dark Side of the Moon*, the list of possibilities was both endless and wry. How appropriate it would be, for example, if after all these years Phish's own repertoire could still be interrupted by Michael Jackson's *Thriller*!

"The Beatles' *White Album* got the most votes," Mike reflects, a total of forty from the four hundred cast. "So we learned that. The songs were simple, but to learn all of them, and all the harmonies in two weeks, it wasn't all that easy. And that was just the second set of a three-set gig. It was a five-and-a-half–hour gig."

Yet for Phish, learning and executing an entire Beatles album could only be a privilege. Mike is adamant. "The Beatles were extremely creative in the studio with songwriting, and I think we all have a lot of respect for that."

Social history, however, has not been kind to the *White Album*. A year after its November 1968 release, a Californian drifter named Charles Manson outbid every psycho who's ever claimed their dog was talking to them by announcing that the Beatles talked to him. He claimed the proof was scattered throughout the band's latest album.

There was "Revolution 9," which became Revelations 9, with Manson as the fifth angel (the first four, of course, were

the Beatles). There was "Sexy Sadie," which Manson understood to be a reference to one of his own disciples, Susan
"Sadie" Atkins. There was "Piggies," which translated into
an indictment of the self-centered capitalists whose society
Manson was ordained to tumble. And most terrifying of all,
there was "Helter Skelter," the doe-eyed Paul McCartney's
playful celebration of a childhood fairground ride, upended
and translated into a manifesto for mass murder.

According to legend, the Beatles' original recording of
"Helter Skelter" was twenty-seven minutes long. According
to another legend, that is how long Manson's killers spent
inside the home of Leno and Rosemary Bianca, whose slaugh-
tered bodies were discovered beneath walls daubed with slo-
gans written in their own blood: "Rise," "Death to Pigs,"
and—proof that the revolution will not necessarily be won by
spelling-bee champions, "Healter Skelter."

A decade later, "Helter Skelter" remained a potent sym-
bol. Siouxsie and the Banshees rerecorded it for their debut
album, *The Scream*, realizing that the Manson connection im-
bued the song with shocking imagery long after punk rock
rendered so much other pop iconography toothless. And
though U2 reappropriated "Helter Skelter" for their own
Rattle and Hum tour, not even Saint Bono's insistence that
Manson stole the song from the Beatles, "but we've come to
take it back," could break the spell. When Guns N' Roses,
the archetypal bad boys of gutter rock 'n' roll, recorded an
album's worth of covers in the early 1990s, there wasn't a U2
song in sight. But there was one by Charles Manson.

Excise Manson from the equation, and the *White Album*
remains a scything experience, a palpable sense of foreboding
leeching through the most harmless grooves, prophesying
both the end of the band and the end of an era. The Beatles
split up as the sixties broke down, just two albums on from
"Bungalow Bill."

For Phish, then, the challenge was not only to re-create the *White Album* in the concert environment where the Beatles never took it (the band retired from live performance a full two years earlier), but to re-create the manifold moods and suggestions that characterized the original album.

The show opened with a snatch of Pink Floyd, just to keep the fans guessing. Then a second tape swelled into life, a recording of Ed Sullivan's immortal introduction of the Beatles to prime-time American television, in February 1964. And from there on in, the *White Album* was re-created in its entirety, song by song, almost note by note, and the only lasting criticism was that in selecting this particular album to xerox, Phish were only highlighting their dexterity. Their personality was lost amid their honesty. "Ob-La-Di, Ob-La-Da," the one song Phish had previously performed (albeit within a jam in Albany eighteen months before), was anonymous enough to pass the karaoke test, and it was not until "While My Guitar Gently Weeps," seven tracks in, that there appeared any palpable sense that here was anything more than a competent Beatles tribute outfit.

Only then could any hint of personal musicianship, Trey's own gymnastic guitar-playing, be unveiled, and one swiftly got the impression that Phish themselves knew this, treating the album's lesser songs as mere bridges toward what Phish themselves viewed as the album's epic numbers. "Sexy Sadie" came in for astonishing treatment; "Helter Skelter," on the other hand, was hamstrung by its own legend, and Phish all but threw it away on a tide of descending bass lines.

Elsewhere, Page's almost-ragtime piano accompaniment to "Martha My Dear" continues to raise a smile even on the generally lower-fi recordings of the show, which went into instant circulation, while a loose "Rocky Raccoon" provides some moments of genuine hilarity, Page unleashing a saloon bar piano perfectly in keeping with the song's subject matter.

A vaguely Presley-flavored and joyfully knockabout take on "Don't Pass Me By" returned the set to more Phish-like essentials, a genuine sense of individuality bleeding through the new arrangement. The same could be said for the near omission of "Birthday," always one of the Beatles' most trite compositions, and reduced by Phish to the simple repetition of a bass line.

A fractious "Yer Blues" fragmented the gentle vibe which was building, and despite the occasional disappointment-to-come, ensured that it never returned. "Yer Blues" was one of the few *White Album* songs to ever escape the confines of its studio presence, as Lennon took it first to the Rolling Stones' *Rock and Roll Circus* extravaganza and then on the road with his Plastic Ono Band, and these are the versions which Phish used as the template for their own, a crunching guitar work-out which came to an end all too quickly.

A beautiful "Cry Baby Cry," pocked by some hesitant vocals but redeemed by the closing guitar solo, offered another of those moments which spoke volumes for Phish's affection for the music they were recounting. But it was "Revolution 9" which proved the surprising revelation. Unrepeatable in its original form, it became a visual, rather than musical, showpiece, Phish performing the manifold sound effects largely unaccompanied, stepping up to the mikes to deliver odd lines in pantomime fashion, and demonstrating, in this dissection of the most controversial track ever placed on a Beatles album, not only how much Lennon borrowed from Frank Zappa (or at least, from the same sources that Frank Zappa borrowed from!), but how much Zappa would later borrow from him.

The set closed, as does the album, with the lilting "Good Night," performed by the Beatles themselves as the house-lights went up. Phish would be performing another set in fifteen minutes, one which would not end until dawn was beginning to break, but already it had been a memorable evening, not to mention an unusual one.

Inside, as the set ended, Chris Kuroda gave himself, and his crew of seven, a silent pat on the back. "I was kind of nervous with the *White Album*," he admitted later. Until Phish actually took the stage, they never even rehearsed the performance with him, and Kuroda admits, "I didn't do too much lighting." But what he did do was great.

Outside, the hardy few hundred who'd turned up ticketless and were mortified to discover the show was sold out weeks in advance, left their jealously guarded places by doors and walls adjoining the auditorium. They'd heard enough to know they'd missed a lot of music and magic, and opportunity as well. As John Paluska commented later, that gig served as a wake-up call to everyone who reckoned Phish were still their own little secret. They were rapidly becoming everyone's.

The tour resumed its normal face the following night, winding toward an incredible triple climax: a Madison Square Garden show (which sold out in a stunning four hours) a debut appearance on the *Late Show with David Letterman*; and, rounding off the year in fine style, Boston Garden on New Year's Eve. In the midst of all that, even a "new" "Phish" album, the Dude of Life's long-delayed but much-anticipated *Crimes of the Mind*, passed by completely unnoticed. Well, almost. *Entertainment Weekly* wrote it off as "inconsequential silliness," and most other nonpartisan listeners concurred.

Tickets for the Boston show were completely sold out in a mere thirty minutes to a jubilant 15,000-strong audience, which was joined by *Rolling Stone* reviewer Paul Robicheau. "Eccentric stage presence and rock-solid musicianship earned Phish their rabid regional following; now the cult has mushroomed beyond all proportion," he marveled. "Without the benefit of radio airplay, this Vermont band sold out Madison

Square Garden the night before New Year's Eve, and then filled its New England home court for this loopy holiday bacchanal."

Once again the aquarium backdrop was the star of the show, although it was quickly upstaged first by the onstage appearance of Mike's grandmother (she would pass away just two weeks later); and then as the wet suit–clad Phish, ably assisted by a team of passing rocket scientists, boarded a giant hot dog and flew out over the crowd with a raucous "Auld Lang Syne."

"That was wild," Mike smiled. "We got on the hot dog and it raised up pretty quickly. It went all the way across Boston Garden to the cheap seats, as they call them. Talk about the feeling of motion while playing; I mean, there we were, actually in a hot dog, moving and playing. Not only that, but it was kosher. We actually had a rabbi come to kosher-fy it."

At least *Rolling Stone* reported that correctly; elsewhere, Robicheau's review claimed the set comprised "mostly unrecorded material," when it actually boiled down to around 50/50, and credited Phish with covering the Beatles' *White Album* in its entirety again. In fact, they didn't play a single Beatles song all night.

There again, it was New Year's Eve.

THAT SHIT IN MY PRESSING ROOM

"It was inevitable," Mike remarked of the forthcoming live Phish album. "It always made sense. But we wanted to wait until we really had the facilities to do it right, the right kind of recording equipment. We wanted to do it a long time ago. The fans have been asking for it for a while. Finally, the way that we decided to do it was by taping every night on thirty-two tracks. So it took two months of listening to our own music to try and pick tracks, and that was tedious but interesting. [Then] we went in the studio and mixed it."

To aid the selection process, the individual group members kept diaries throughout the tour, noting their own favorite gigs. Every show that at least two musicians cited then went onto a master list, a process which whittled the initial number of songs down to a mere 560. From there, it was a matter of ruthlessly cutting the roster to one hundred songs, then to thirty, and finally to the eleven which could be fit onto a two-CD set.

The Phish Net also played a part in this process, as Phish strove to establish the ultimate balance, between album favorites and unreleased gems, between their own preferred performances and the audience's personal highlights. The final running order proved the wisdom of such a compromise.

Although the sleeve itself gives the impression that the album was recorded live at just one superlative gig, Phish did in fact cull tracks from ten different shows: Pittsburgh (10/9/94); Bangor, Maine (11/2/94); University of Michigan (11/16/94); Minneapolis (11/26/94); Montana State University (11/28/94); Davis, California (12/2/94); San Diego (12/7/94); Santa Monica (12/10/94); Madison Square Garden (12/30/94); and one that no amount of scrutiny of existing concert tapes has been able to pin down.

They also pulled a stunning version of "Stash" from an FM broadcast of their Great Woods show on July 8. Then, with Elektra having been persuaded to slash the normal retail price of a double CD to a bargain $19.95, *A Live One* was scheduled for release on June 27, 1995. Phish would begin their own touring schedule three weeks before that.

Even with the band off the road, of course, the Phish Net continued to buzz with excitement, reaching a crescendo at the end of March, when the Memphis grapevine let on that Phish would be opening for the Dead on the first day of April. More people fell for that tale than a quick look at the date should have allowed. In fact, Phish would not be sighted until mid-May, when they finally emerged from a new year spent preparing *A Live One*, to play a benefit for Voters for Choice.

The gig was John Paluska's idea. Five months earlier, an activist claiming to represent the anti-abortion lobby had shot and killed two nurses working at local Boston clinics. A number of other clinics were revealed to have been targeted by fanatics; Paluska lived next door to one of them. For Phish, whose own long-standing policy of avoiding political benefits was only one of the things they were placing at risk, the die was cast almost before the show was even scheduled.

The benefit was not an experience they relished. Fish told

Relix, "We did it, and then we got a lot of mail from some pro-life people, not fanatic people, like the ones who blow up hospitals, not even religious people. And I found a lot of their arguments rational. If I had stood onstage and said what I thought, it would have been different from what the people who were running that thing said."

He was particularly disturbed by a backstage "Wall of Shame" which pictured various anti-abortionist politicians and captioned them "evil." "Maybe these guys had a personal reason to be anti-abortion," Fish mused. "That doesn't necessarily mean these people are evil. I didn't ask for that shit in my dressing room! I am supporting the right for a person to make a choice, I don't like the 'us and them' mentality."

Unfortunately, such apparent common sense itself placed Fish, if not Phish, firmly within one of those camps. In emotive issues like this, there is no middle ground.

Phish's 1995 summer tour opened in Boise, Idaho, on June 7, three weeks before *A Live One* was due in the shops. The timing was frustrating for the fans for whom a pre-gig discussion of recent events was a key element of the concert experience. But it was of no concern whatsoever to the vast numbers of Newbies who now sent Phish spiraling into much the same ballpark as the post–*Touch of Gray* Dead. The only difference was, Phish hadn't yet racked up a hit single. Where were all these people coming from, then? And more important, what were they going to do? After the Madison Square Garden sellout, John Paluska, bristling with pride, nevertheless offered up a suggestion of caution. "Phish is like hot coals," he observed. "The last thing we want is a brush fire."

They got one anyway.

On June 23, with *A Live One* looming, Phish played Waterloo Village, in Stanhope, New Jersey. Waterloo Village itself boasts the grim countenance of an Eastern European tractor factory, the kind of place which Ukrainian tour guides used to point out with such pride. The organization surrounding it, however, wouldn't have lasted five minutes in the former Soviet Union. "Are [shows at the venue] always that disorganized?" one Internet user asked afterward. "We waited to get on a bus from seven-thirty till nine-thirty and missed the whole first set. I would have walked the five miles had I known how difficult it would have been to take the shuttle."

Another did walk, into a hail of glass bottles being thrown from a passing bus. And a third, a fan named Daniel Malone, hitched a ride on a passing car, fell, and was killed.

Afterward, the local Mount Olive police department appeared to wash its hands of the tragedy, informing the media that Malone, like hundreds of other fans making their way to the venue, deliberately chose to endanger himself by not waiting for a bus. According to them, Malone was not the only person who clambered aboard a moving vehicle to try and beat the system; the marvel was that he was the only one who was killed. "But if you were there," *Pharmer's Almanac* contributor Andy Bernstein condemned, "you know there were no buses available, and hundreds of cars did not even make it to the parking lots, because highway exits were needlessly blocked off."

Bernstein's were sentiments with which many other Phish fans agreed. Wholly unprepared for an invasion of this size, Waterloo did not appear to rise to the challenge of safely, and competently, policing the converging fans. The highway was jammed by parked and abandoned cars. Satellite parking lots were cut off, transport was at an absolute standstill. For 16,000 fans who'd dropped in excess of $25 per ticket and entertained no intention of missing a minute of music, the cars that were still moving offered the only feasible way of making it to the venue.

Inside the venue, the audience's palpable unrest was contagious. Onstage, too, there was friction, as Phish—accompanied by John Popper—launched into an appropriate cover of Abba's "Waterloo," then ended it with unimaginable abruptness. "I kind of liked that," Mike raved afterward, but Trey didn't. "He ended it in the middle."

Devastated as they were by the news of Malone's death, Phish continued the tour by begging their fans to follow whatever instructions they were given by venue or police authorities, even if it did mean missing shows. A few hours of music—even the greatest music in the world—could never be more important than life and limb.

Paluska's feared brush fire, however, was in no mood to listen. A three-hour traffic jam on the approach to Great Woods saw a near repeat of the chaos which attended Waterloo, as fans simply abandoned their vehicles and trudged the last few miles of highway.

Nor was there any relief from the bedlam as they reached the arena. Ticketless fans, fondly remembering the days when one Phish Head would happily miracle another and spare tickets could be gleaned for five bucks, a couple of joints, or nothing more than a smile and a thank you, clogged the parking lot. Local kids, not part of this scene at all, but knowing full well that where there are crowds there's action, followed suit.

For many people, Great Woods was the first chance to compare notes since *A Live One* was released and *Rolling Stone* began to accord Phish a modicum of the attention they merited, awarding *A Live One* three stars in a rating system of five. The debate was audible all through the hall.

"Noodlers," writer Tom Moon called Phish, and "probably the most self-indulgent act ever to sell out Madison Square Garden." *A Live One*, therefore, was "a noodler manifesto, the definitive statement of the jam-band aesthetic," and the band's songs, already dismissed as "determinedly adolescent music distinguished by outbreaks of fey vocal non-sense," weren't songs at all, they were simply "platforms for noodling."

It was actually a fairly funny review, as funny as those jabs the English press used to make at Yes at the height of their pomp-and-circumstance posturing, circa *Tales from Topographic Oceans*. In fact, Phish shared several of *Rolling Stone*'s reservations. Mike admitted, "We're critical of *A Live One*. We think it's kind of long-winded."

But Phish fans aren't always renowned for their sense of humor, and Shell McLennan, still supporting the group after six years of touring, insists that some of them aren't even sure what humor is.

Yet humor is integral to the band's very being. Phish, like Frank Zappa, flirt with a musical irony which one is often hard-pressed to define; which is, by definition, so archly un-American that any notions of domestic success which its perpetrators might harbor must be balanced automatically against the knowledge that most of their target audience won't comprehend half of what they're listening to.

Zappa himself understood this conflict intuitively, and spent at least the first five years of his mainstream musical career poking fun at the very people who were buying his music in the belief that it was something else—art, maybe, or simply something so obtuse that the very possession of *Hot Rats* or *Weasels Ripped My Flesh* conveyed a kind of mystic superiority upon their owner.

Phish tempered their obtuseness from the very beginning; having started life as a virtual covers outfit, they intended going to the grave with their fingers still in that pie, recognizing that even in the depths of delicious obscurity, the most knuckleheaded onlooker would get some kind of charge out of "Highway to Hell."

But would they also get the joke? Apparently not.

Still reeling from the below-the-belt blow of Waterloo Village; aware that the brush fire was already scorching the scrubland and getting dangerously close to the property line, Phish loaded up the three buses and four equipment trucks which now hauled their entourage around, and headed toward their fall tour with renewed caution.

Word of mouth continued to increase Phish's mainstream visibility, however, with a second well-received appearance on the David Letterman show, just seven months after their first, thus taking care of any stragglers who'd missed hearing them elsewhere.

Fortuitously timed as if to counter the rush, the long-promised Phish Tickets by Mail hotline—offering choice seats with minimal overheads—clicked into place, but its evolution was slow, and its successes short-lived. And it was still accompanied by the caveat that would become as much a mantra for John Paluska as it ever was for the Grateful Dead: If you don't have tickets, don't come to the show. Of course his words fell on deaf ears, but he needed to be seen doing something—and short of pulling Phish off the road altogether, what else could he do?

In fact the tour started sedately, even sparsely. The vast Cal Expo Amphitheater in Sacramento positively echoed to the sound of a half-capacity audience, while outside, security swooped upon the unauthorized vendors with their balloons and their baubles, clearing the parking lot before many of them even made their first sale.

T-shirt salesmen scattered, the homemade-jewelry hawkers, anybody who could be remotely perceived as fleecing the fans, regardless of their motives, was sent hastily packing, and, by the stage door afterward, at least one pair of Phish Heads bemoaned their sorry fate.

They'd spent four years traveling in the wake of Phish,

financing their travels and tickets by selling the necklaces and earrings they'd made between tours. The new-look clampdown ensured they'd either have to stop traveling, or they'd start taking risks, hitchhiking instead of riding the Greyhounds; turning up ticketless instead of booking months in advance. By ridding themselves of the most visible eyesores, a dreadlocked boy defiantly snarled, Phish were simply opening the doors to far more pernicious problems. Hell still hath no fury like the loyal fan scorned.

What made matters even worse was that it wasn't Phish themselves who were opening that door, it was the corporate giants of Giant, to whom they'd contracted their merchandising.

Bootleg merchandising has long been the bane of the touring scene, and dealing with heavy responses to it was likewise part and parcel of being a Head. In 1993 the Grateful Dead went so far as to file lawsuits in seven states against illegal merchandisers, citing everything from T-shirts "and other clothing items, to stickers, posters, and lyric books," all of which, a subsequent press release warned, "were seized pursuant to Federal Court seizure orders and under local anti-counterfeiting and anti-vending laws.

"Additionally, a Federal Court . . . entered a $15,000 judgment (which was stayed by agreement) and permanent injunction against a defendant (with much harsher penalties should he violate the injunction) against the sale of unauthorized [Dead] videotapes."

The logic behind the action was, If the Grateful Dead want to put out a T-shirt, a sticker or a whatever, only the Dead have a right to do so, and to determine and assure the content and quality. Now Phish were moving down that same road.

Andy Bernstein, one of the brains behind the ever-popular but distinctly unofficial "Goin' Phishin' " tour shirts, remembers one particular run-in with the Phish organization. "Amy told [us] the band hated our shirts, that they wanted the 'Goin' Phishin' shirts 'off the lot.' Those were their words. And that bummed us out, because we always said we'd never do anything to piss off the band."

To hear that Phish disapproved of his activities really hurt, so after the show, Bernstein and his partner waited around until Page boarded the tour bus, then cornered him. "We asked what the deal was . . . 'If you want us to stop [selling the shirts] just say so.' He looked at us kind of puzzled. 'Why would we want you to stop?' "

A couple of nights later, Bernstein saw Mike Gordon wade into a similar fray, taking the T-shirt sellers' side against his own organization. Yet even Phish, it seemed, were powerless to halt the corporate juggernaut around them. It was as though the band's associates believed that if decisions were left to Phish themselves, the kids would get away with anything. So a protective armor fell into place around the group. What had once been keeping them safe was now keeping them prisoner.

One evening, the security team removed Andy Bernstein and his partner from the venue as soon as they got inside. "We would have been really bummed," Bernstein wrote afterward, "had Mike Gordon not walked right up to us after the show and said he was sorry, that if it was up to him, we would have been in there."

Yet it was the same story every night, every tour, for so many of the vendors who once trailed Phish, around the country. In San Diego, though, ticketless hopefuls were at least repaid for ignoring Paluska's mandate, when they turned up on the off chance, and discovered tickets remained on sale right up until showtime. There was even time to relax in the sunshine, as well, and listen as Phish ran through a dynamic soundcheck: "Gumbo," "All Things Reconsidered,"

"Mound," and a brand-new song which seemed to be called "Ragtime Girl."

With just a three-month-old collection of in-concert staples to promote, it was no surprise that Phish opted to use their 1995 winter tour as an excuse to break in a host of new songs, road-testing possibilities for their next album, next year.

"Taste," debuted earlier in the season and now mutating toward its final identity as "The Fog That Surrounds," arrived early in the set; so did Page's "Cars, Trucks and Buses" and the sweeping "Keyboard Calvary." There was an airing for "Billy Breathes," a song Trey wrote for his newborn daughter Eliza, nicknamed Billy for who knows what reason, and at the Greek Theater in Los Angeles, Fish gleefully massacred Aerosmith's "Cryin'," admitting to the hysterical audience, "I don't really know the words to this song. But that isn't the point."

Another massacre got under way the following night, at the Shoreline Amphitheater. Phish were no more than three songs into the set, launching into a jam that no one on the floor recognized, when suddenly a monster chess set descended from the ceiling. With the band's then-current monitor engineer Pete Schall calling the shots, it was band versus fans, a veritable battle of the giants.

Phish made the first move, and the board disappeared; the fans would take their turn early into the second set, moving a piece by the consensus of a hurried conference at the Greenpeace stall. Then the game returned to the heavens, to be continued another night. Two games were completed that tour; Phish won the first, checkmating 4,314 fans at the Tampa Sun Dome on November 15; the fans won the second, when Phish resigned onstage at Madison Square Garden, that New Year's Eve.

On through the itinerary. Phish sold out Spokane, Missoula, Tempe. . . . Austin, home of the annual South-by-Southwest (SXSW) alternative-music seminar, raced past in another blur, most memorable for the punk kids in the parking lot, with what sounded like a tape loop of a local punk combo, the Hormones, steaming through Bowie's "John, I'm Only Dancing." Phish retaliated with "David Bowie" itself; two nights earlier, they'd brought his "Life on Mars?" into the set for the first time. There was obviously some very weird karma being worked out that evening, which was fitting because there was some very weird music being made onstage as well.

Nobody knew what to make of Phish's special guests that night, the Medeski, Martin and Wood trio, who had wandered out of New York City's "downtown" jazz scene, but were now better known for their tropical sanctuary, a self-sufficient recording studio in a Hawaiian shack.

It was true, of course, that MMW drew their inspiration from many of the same roots as Phish—Jimmy Smith, Sun Ra, Miles Davis—and according to John Medeski, they adapted those roots in the same way, too. "We take the grooves and harmonic concepts that are natural to us, and stretch them the way that we can through improvisation." But, he also concedes, "We may be expressing something different than what most pop shoots for. We're trying to bring the aesthetic of jazz down to earth for younger generations to relate to."

In Atlanta, they may or may not have succeeded, but Trey, at least, was amazed. "We had this incredible twenty-five-minute jam with both bands, with this screaming peak where everyone was running around the stage at a full sprint, and shit was buzzing all over the place. And when we got to New Orleans three days later, we decided to go for it again."

Through Missouri, Iowa, Nebraska, Wisconsin—through the great midwest of America's dreaming. It was raining, chilly, misty, on October 31, 1995, as the caravan pulled into Rosemont, that last bastion of civilization on the fringe of Chicago. But even early in the day, it appeared strangely altered, as though somewhere along I-90 reality slipped a notch and suddenly the dour wasteland separating one of America's largest cities from the world's largest airport was simply another part of the saga of Gamehendge.

The theater was awash with sound and color, packed to the rafters and swinging from them, too. The air of expectation was more than palpable; you could have cut it with a knife and played it on CD. The Halloween costumes were out in full force, and the Phish birthday suits mingled with the crowd. A few people tried to predict which album Phish would be recapturing onstage tonight; one year on from the *White Album*, Phish had again polled the fans, collecting the votes together, and onstage they were in festive spirits, knowing they knew something the audience didn't.

"Icculus" opened the evening's set, and all around, they could sense the historians flicking through the dog-eared *Helping Friendly Books* which they carried around in their heads, trying to determine just when the song was last played (November 20, 1994, in Madison, Wisconsin); where in the set it usually fell (between "Colonel Forbin's Ascent" and "Famous Mockingbird," its rightful place in the Gamehendge saga); and whether it had ever opened a Phish set before (no way).

Through "Ya Mar," the soporific Caribbean calypso gone crazy, and "Sparkle"; and with every old friend, the crowd roared as another handful of people raised themselves above the melee, bowed, and indicated their costumes: "This one's all about *me*."

Dressing up was such a ritual, so integral but organic a part of the Phish experience. But watching them, it was hard not to think about the guy dressed as Buffalo Bill; what a hopeless life of hope he must be leading. But if the group played that song, he would wet himself with joy. It must be dreadful to be the one person whose chosen persona never made it onstage, who turned up for every show in such high hopes, then left, disappointed one more time. A few aisles away, there was a woman dressed as a baby, with "Bundle of Joy" sewn onto her chest. Phish hadn't played her song in over six years.

"Free," just five months old but welcomed like a conquering hero, confirmed its status as the greatest rock song to employ a cowbell since the Stones first met those "Honky-Tonk Women." A mammoth "Guyute" bled into "Harpua," and while the band jammed on, Trey started telling a story, something about a boy named Jimmy, the hero of the song, who was sitting around listening to "the very same album that Phish will be playing as their Halloween album at the Rosemont Horizon." And then they broke into "Beat It."

Yes, *that* "Beat It." Michael Jackson's "Beat It." The "Beat It" that told the debutante Phish what to do, twelve years before at an ROTC dance. Roars of acknowledgment from one half of the crowd, chuckles of derision from the other; they were in on the joke, they knew the old story, but even their smiles began to fade when Phish emerged for their second set, and the prerecorded rhythms of another Jackson thriller, "Wanna Be Starting Something" echoed over their heads. Then, before anyone could really spoil it, and point out that they'd done the same sort of thing last year, coming out onstage to *Dark Side of the Moon*, every other sound in the room was drowned by the roar of the wind and the crash of the sea.

"The story is set . . . on a rock . . . in the middle of a stormy sea."

Quadrophenia was Pete Townshend's masterpiece. Other Who albums have their fans, others are built around better songs, stronger performances, more dynamic music. But if Townshend's ouvre was to create a seamless blending of story and song, with an underlying philosophy and an overwhelming intensity, *Quadrophenia*—as befits its title—is a four-way showcase for all that made the Who truly special, the last of their albums to even make that attempt, and the first to actually succeed.

Running the gamut of musical moods for which the Who justly became famous, from pounding semi-metal ("The Punk and the Godfather") to impassioned balladeering (the closing "Love Reign O'er Me"), from fifties-style rock 'n' roll ("5:15") to folky jig-a-jigging ("The Rock"), *Quadrophenia* was not only the last significant album of the Who's own career, it was conceivably also the first significant album of the late 1970s—and that despite being released a full three years before even the Sex Pistols had heard of punk rock.

The double album *Quadrophenia* appeared in the United States in October 1973, but the British release was dogged by production problems, and when the Who took the stage for the first live performance of this new magnum opus, at Stoke's Trentham Gardens, *Quadrophenia* was still pending. The show was as chaotic as the audience's reaction, almost two hours of new material when all you really want are the hits, and the following night in Wolverhampton, the Who didn't even attempt to perform the entire album.

the Who's customarily spontaneous live set was thrown completely out by the need to play along with the prerecorded tapes which *Quadrophenia*'s dynamics demanded, and by the fourth night of the British tour, in Manchester, the band was dropping five new songs from the show. They were contemplating cutting more when, finally, disaster struck.

On November 5, 1973, the British holiday which is so appropriately known as "Fireworks Night" to millions of schoolchildren, soundman Bobby Pridden jumped the gun with one of the cues and set one of the tapes rolling too early.

In front of a packed Newcastle Odeon, Townshend exploded. Dragging Pridden away from the sound desk, and sending an amplifier sprawling in the process, he proceeded to attack the tape machines, wrecking weeks of work in a matter of seconds. Pridden quit on the spot (although he was persuaded to return later that night), and after a thirty-minute cooling-off period, the Who ended their set with a solid greatest-hits routine, culminating with Townshend smashing his guitar to smithereens. Fireworks Night indeed!

It would be another twenty-two years before Townshend and the Who felt confident enough to return *Quadrophenia* to the stage, a massive theatrical presentation which they debuted in London in June 1996. Phish beat them to it by nearly eight months, but it was almost three minutes before the audience even pretended to know what was going on. Then the first vocal lines cut through the wind and waves: *"Can you see the real me—can you . . . can you?"*

Quadrophenia actually finished second on the fan base's poll, behind Zappa's *Joe's Garage*, but if anybody objected to Phish rigging the vote, they were maintaining their own silent counsel. "I think of it like the electoral college in the presidentials," laughs Shell McLennan. "We all get to vote, but we're not really the ones who are choosing who wins."

"I liked it," Chris Kuroda told interviewer Dean Budnick. "I enjoyed it a lot. *Quadrophenia* was [an album] I listened to a million times, drilled it in my head." He revealed that Phish actually rehearsed the entire performance in an empty arena before taking it to the Rosemont, "and I got to play around so I was ready for that. I always feel better when I'm ready."

Whatever problems the Who used to have with *Quadro-*

phenia, time and technology clearly rendered obsolete. Over the intro tapes, "The Real Me" exploded into life, the stage ablaze with lights, the horn section—Dave Grippo, Don Glasco, Alan Parchley, and Trey's cousin, Joe Somerville—making its presence felt within moments, and Trey himself launching himself into space again and again, as though the flailing windmill arm he'd borrowed from classic Townshend could actually help him defy gravity.

At first, the tight structure of *Quadrophenia* didn't really suit Phish. Just as the Who learned when they first tried staging their dynamic extravaganza, the need for prerecorded tapes ensured there was less room for improvisation, less space in which to maneuver, and let the music go where it wanted to. Slowly, though, they came to grips with it all, introducing little musical asides so you knew it wasn't Memorex: "Helpless Dancer," with its speed-vocal shenanigans excusing Phish the political incorrectness of Townshend's original lyric; or "I've Had Enough," with Mike on banjo, Fish on washboard, and Page on upright bass—a genuine fifties skiffle lineup playing a genuine seventies interpretation of genuine sixties teenage angst. That's not a combination you find every day!

Then it was into the closing stretch, a riotous "Bell Boy," with a real live red-suited bell boy emerging to scurry back and forth across the stage; an impassioned "Dr. Jimmy," sauntering arrogance and youthful disdain bleeding from every lyric; and a squawking, chattering, horn-powered transition into "The Rock," truly one of the most unself-consciously joyous moments in the Who's entire catalog.

Phish played it dead straight, but that didn't matter. The audience itself was enraptured, lost, consumed by the song's natural pounding rhythm, that timeless bopping hopscotch for the senses, 18,000 people grinning idiotically, clapping, bouncing, willing the band to keep on going even when it was inevitable that the song was almost over.

With Trey moving over to drums, and Page's pure piano fit to break your heart, Fish took lead vocals for "Love Reign O'er Me," the soaring finale to the drama before. He isn't the best singer in the group's ranks, and the song deserved better, but the crowd took him with them regardless, as if willpower alone could iron out the kinks. And so Quadrophenia went out on a surging, if slightly off-key, note.

Forty minutes of a "You Enjoy Myself" jam, interludes taking the song everywhere but to bed . . . ZZ Top's "Jesus Just Left Chicago," driving Texan rhythm and blues . . . a triumphant "A Day in the Life." Phish had the bit in their teeth now, slammed into a passionate, virtuoso "Suzy Greenberg," and that was it . . . almost.

A jokey, acoustic bluegrass return to the Who songbook brought an encore of "My Generation," not award-winning musically, but supersonic visually, as Trey's acoustic guitar met its maker on the stage, and Fish's drum kit was kicked out and toppled. Then, while Page on bass and Mike on banjo continued playing away, Trey swept the debris to the back of the stage and blew the whole pile to pieces.

WE NEED TO PURIFY THE BODY

And still the road went on forever, until the blasted heaths of Astroturf all blended into each other, buffeted by the blast of a thousand moisture-draining extractor fans. If, as Andy Warhol once quipped, everyone's a star for fifteen minutes, then this entire tour was about to become an extra in some twisted, hippie *Macbeth*: Eye of newt and dead man's hand—buy them hot from the hot-dog stand. Despite the cold, the crowd wore the smug expression of people who'd overheard Coco Chanel at a floor show, and thought that the wisdom was directed at him: "Fashions come and go, but style is here to stay." The trouble was, in that sea of tie-dye and bellbottoms and beads, this style had arrived in 1967 and hadn't washed its armpits since. It wasn't going to start now, either.

In death, as in life, Jerry Garcia would not leave Phish alone. The Grand Old Man of jamming checked out on August 9, 1995, and Fish, for one, could not believe what he'd been hearing since then. "Everyone was saying, 'God, you guys are really gonna go over the top now!' And I kept saying, 'I really don't think that's gonna happen.'"

What was worse, most people meant it as a compliment,

as though Garcia's very existence was somehow keeping Phish from fulfilling their true destiny. Even *Relix*, a magazine that owed its very existence to the Dead, seemed to be somehow passing the baton over to Phish, retaining them as the magazine's latest cover stars even after the Garcia story broke and hearts broke with it. "This issue was nearly completed when the news hit," *Relix* publisher Toni A. Brown wrote, "[and] after searching my heart for days, I decided to leave the majority of the issue . . . intact. To change covers seemed almost exploitative."

Fish concurred with her intentions. "There is no next Garcia," he would insist, and even if there were, Phish were hardly likely to be lining up to meet him. As *Mojo* magazine's Barney Hoskyns pointed out a year later, "The Dead are merely one of several tributaries that flow into Phish's river. Zappa and Steely Dan are just as evident . . . while a fixation with the late great Sun Ra remains a potent inspiration."

Regardless, the comparisons with the Dead would keep mounting up, or at least self-perpetuating, beginning with the oft-fired complaint that Phish were first and foremost a live outfit. This in turn implied they'd never make the record they were capable of, until they made a live one. Now that they'd done that, the comparisons could move to the next level. Like the day Trey Anastasio recorded his first solo album.

"One morning," he remembered, "I literally woke up with the complete idea for [an] album, the musicians I wanted, and the sound I was looking for. I ran downstairs and started making calls." He ended up spending two days inside Electric Ladyland Studios, with a coterie of fellow conspirators which *Unbroken Chain* would describe as "a roster which is to improvisatory jazz and rock what the Dream Team is to basketball."

This was not the first time Trey reached outside of the confines of Phish; over the last couple of years, he and Fish had frequently relaxed with mandolin player Jamie Masefield and bassist Stacey Starkweather, playing shows around New England under the names the Jazz Mandolin Project, and later, Bad Hat.

And *Surrender to the Air* was never going to be a Trey Anastasio album per se, even though it was his dream, his vision, his attempt "to capture the music I've been hearing in my head." Rather, it was a vast musical cooperative, its members credited on the album cover in strict alphabetical order (Trey came second, after saxophonist Marshall Allen), and the loose musical ideas for which Trey took credit were adapted by them into a sprawl of improvisations which ran, again in the words of *Unbroken Chain*, from "soft jazzy textures to heavy, dissonant crashing . . . thunderous cacophony to silky grooves."

Surrender to the Air was self-indulgent, of course, but for Trey, it was also somewhat therapeutic. Phish had hit a wall, he admitted to *Guitar Player* magazine. "My reaching the point of wanting to get this album out is symbolic of where all four of us are. We fell into the trap of forgetting where the bare truth is. We've crossed that line, now we're moving toward a void, ready to jump."

It was no secret that Elektra were very disappointed with *Hoist*, even though it had proven Phish's best-selling album yet; nor that the label viewed *A Live One* as a conciliatory gesture and a stop-gap hole filler. Neither was it any secret that *Surrender to the Air* was best regarded as an outlet for tendencies Trey might have otherwise attempted to foist onto Phish's own next album.

"Phish has been my main focus for twelve years," Trey agreed, "and this album is an idea I've had in the back of my mind for a long time and was really excited to finally get to do. I feel as good about it as anything I've ever been involved with.

"A lot of people have criticized me and Phish—'How come you do bluegrass for a section of your show, and then fugues, and then Jack Johnson jazz? Make up your mind!' I've never been able to. With this, I was trying to put the intense limits of each thing into a piece where nothing repeats. That blast at the beginning goes into the funky 'We Deflate,' then a Latin section, then the duet with [guitarist Marc] Ribot, then meterless piano with guitars in the backgrounds. . . ." And so on.

Ribot, Allen, Damon R. Choice, and Michael Ray (of Sun Ra's Arkestra); John Medeski of Medeski, Martin and Wood; Oteil and Kofi Burbridge of the Aquarium Rescue Unit; Bob Gulloti; Phish's own Jon Fishman . . . "I have the greatest respect for all these musicians," Trey drooled. "It was a thrill to be in the same room as them"—and an even greater thrill to reconvene them for two nights at the Academy theater in New York City, at the beginning of April 1996.

With Page McConnell guesting through the second night's last set, and trombonist James Harvey joining the party for the night, a packed house thrilled to a truly democratic display: *Dupree's Diamond News* was only one of the magazines to comment on Trey's own utter lack of ego, as Marc Ribot, a veteran of stints with Tom Waits and Elvis Costello, took total control of the guitar leads department. But the occasion was such that the combined virtuosity more than outweighed personal predilections. They could remain on hold for another couple of weeks, until Phish descended upon New Orleans.

Phish hit the 27th Annual New Orleans Jazz and Heritage Festival like a racehorse at the winning post. Spread over ten glorious days of music, food, and relentless humidity, the festival is one of the jewels in New Orleans' cultural crown, yet Phish's inclusion in the bill, playing their first scheduled live show of 1996, and their last until the August tour kicked off, saw the Louisiana Fairgrounds Racetrack swamped like never before.

"The Phish Heads have taken over the place," reported *Musician* magazine. "Fleets of Volkswagen buses run through the French Quarter, and the shores of the Mississippi throng with tie-dyed kids selling homemade necklaces for cash to get to the next town."

"For anyone who hasn't gone to Jazzfest," Mike raved, "there's like sixty bands a day and that's just at the festival. Then there are all the clubs. One of our favorite things to do, after we play, is to go out to different clubs and to see music and to meet other musicians with different ethnic backgrounds. If music has passion and is being made with the right intent, then we like to check it out and maybe be inspired by it. Hopefully, with our fans, they have that same attitude."

Sadly, they didn't. According to most reports, many fans were so disinterested in the proceedings that they missed what other, less partisan observers considered to be one of the highlights of the festival, when Trey joined Cajun harpist Sunpie Barnes and the Louisiana Sunspots onstage the day after Phish themselves played. And that same evening, both the indefatigable guitarist and Page were recruited for both sets of Michael Ray and the Cosmic Krewe's show at the uptown club Jimmy's.

"It's flattering that we were asked to play," Trey acknowledged. "For me, of all the festivals, Jazzfest is the top of the list. And the music that it's all about has influenced all of us so strongly, so I think we fit in all right."

Phish played early in the afternoon on the first day, exploding onto the Ray·Ban Stage with what could only be described as a version of "When the Saints Come Marching In," cunningly disguised as a breezy "Ya Mar." "AC/DC Bag,"

"Sparkle," and "Stash" all followed, before the band was joined onstage by Michael Ray, adding trumpet and percussion to a wild, funky "Cars, Trains and Buses."

"Also Sprach Zarathustra," later in the show, maintained the funkiness, but if the remainder of the set threatened to switch into overdrive, as "You Enjoy Myself," "Scent of a Mule," and "Harry Hood" sandwiched the genuine highlights, Phish still carried some surprises in store. "A Day in the Life" and "David Bowie" wrapped up the show before the encores, an a cappella "Ragtime Gal" and a blistering "Cavern."

The show was a triumph, but George Wein, the festival's executive producer, was adamant afterward. "Phish will not be invited back." The *Los Angeles Times* added what Wein didn't say: The record-breaking attendance of 62,000 might have been great for the festival, but left a distinctly sour taste in the mouths of the locals. The already-troubled French Quarter overflowed with out-of-towners—kids, one local merchant complained, who were "just a step up from gutter punks."

Phish fans, it was reported, clogged the streets and blocked pathways in the festival, pissed where they wanted to, and slept everywhere else. They didn't have time for anything other than Phish, they panhandled visitors and city folk alike, and they walked their puppies everywhere.

Jason Colton, Dionysian's media officer, was amazed at the complaints. "We take great pains to make sure our fans don't leave an impact on a community," he insisted. New Orleans, he continued, was the first time he ever heard of Phish fans making themselves unwelcome. It wouldn't be the last.

In July 1996, Phish returned to Europe for the first time in four years. "Our big dream . . . we actually talked about not putting it out to the mailing list at all," Trey confessed.

"We knew that as soon as we announced the shows, there'd be all these folks that would come over, but we wanted to be put in front of an audience that didn't know us."

In the event, the few hundred ardent Phish Heads who decided to spend a summer in Europe following Phish were a welcome sight amid audiences for whom Phish was just a peculiarly named support group; a welcome sight which Phish rewarded at a hastily scheduled show in Nuremberg by dedicating a brand-new song to the hardy travelers—"The Train Song." After all, aside from three other shows, in London, Amsterdam, and Hamburg, where Phish headlined their own gigs, the real draw on the tour was Carlos Santana.

"It's really wonderful touring with Santana again," Trey enthused, and as he and Carlos resumed their onstage jams, he added, "I really like playing with them because those guys are so nice." In the French city of Arles, on Carlos's forty-ninth birthday, even hardened Phish Heads admitted that few concert experiences could match the spectacle of the two outfits uniting for a twenty-five-minute blast through Sly Stone's "Dance to the Music" and "I Want to Take You Higher."

Relix quoted one fan, a local artisan named Mohamed Touloum: "Santana began their show, played about three songs, then [Trey] and [Mike] came out, they were jamming like twenty, twenty-five minutes. And it was a great, great jam. Everyone was really crazy. It reminded me a little bit of a Dead show. You could see that feeling between the people and the band was so great. And when Phish arrived on the stage, they put it higher. Soon we had two basses, two guitars, two keyboards, Phish's drummer, the other drummers, and the congas. For me, it's been a long time since I saw a show like that."

Audiences, too, reacted well to the bizarre spectacle with which they'd been presented. "Being the opening act," Fish mused, "I felt like I was just starting to appreciate the moment, like in the 'Bike Song' jam, really just looking at what was in front of us, and them looking at us, and you really start to get a feel for that. It's just the funniest thing when you can get into a weird moment, because we don't have that back home. We have an audience that accepts us and knows us, and we don't get into a lot of situations like that."

Some things, however, didn't change. *Relix*, along for the ride when the tour hit Paris, pointed out that the evening's venue, Le Zenith, was also the scene of the Dead's last French show, back in October 1990, a fact which "served to resurrect the inevitable Dead-Phish comparisons." The massed ranks of French Deadheads who turned up to check out these latest claimants to the Dead throne only added to the sense of déjà vu, and journalist Phil Demetrion experienced no difficulty sniffing out local witnesses. "It was like home," Deadhead Eric Cougrand told him. "like a Dead show. I know Phish Heads are often Deadheads, and that Deadheads are not Phish Heads, but this was like the Dead tour here in 1990."

Unfortunately, such connotations were not rooted solely in peace and love, as Phish discovered when they arrived home and set out on the road again.

Long before Phish blew into Colorado, for their now-annual celebration at Red Rocks, the police and Dionysian Productions issued their customary plea that ticketless fans stay away from the venue. The year before, security guards had pumped tear gas into the crowd to try and calm the ticketless fans, and as a similar caravan prepared to make that same journey, hoping that they'd find a way in somehow, all eyes were alert to the possibility of a more organized break-in. It was an age-old game, and it usually passed off without incident.

This time, though, the police weren't simply mouthing platitudes. Every person entering the Red Rocks parking lot was asked to produce a valid concert ticket, and the security teams weren't above conducting on-the-spot searches, hunting for ticketless fans trying to sneak in under seats and in trunks.

Outside the official parking lots, Highway 74 was jammed with parked and deserted vehicles. The Chief Hosa campground was overflowing twenty-four hours before Phish were even due on-site. And still security did the rounds, demanding tickets and evicting anyone they didn't believe had a right to be there.

Frustrated, angry, bored, the ticketless masses, three or four thousand of them by some estimates, descended upon Morrison, the town nearest the amphitheater. More police arrived. Sensing trouble, local businesses put up the shutters and closed for the day. It was an old, old story, if not one whose ramifications could be dulled by repetition. Two years before, similar circumstances saw a riot explode at the Dead's spring-tour stop in Orlando, while the increasing incidence of attempted gate-crashing left the entire Deadhead community on edge.

In those instances, the hardcore fans desperately tried damage limitation, insisting it wasn't true Dead fans, but local rowdies intent on partying whatever the cost, who caused the trouble, and maybe it was. Maybe it was that same element who blasted Morrison, Colorado, too. But hot on the heels of New Orleans, which itself followed Waterloo with such indecent haste, clearly there was cause for concern.

The trouble started in the most bizarre way. A twenty-one-year-old female pedestrian on Morrison's downtown Bear Creek Road was knocked down by a pickup truck, a hit-and-run which the emergency services were swift to respond to. Not, however, as swift as the crowd of kids who gathered around and announced they would heal the woman holistically.

It was literally a scene straight out of a parents' worse

nightmare; either that, or a ghastly psychedelic cliché. When the police tried to break through the crowd, they were physically stopped. "We need to purify the body," somebody demanded.

"And we need to get through now." The police, baffled but becoming increasingly and understandably belligerent, continued trying to shove through; they were met with bottles. Things simply snowballed from there. Without warning, a gathering of Phish fans erupted into the kind of running melee which the media would swiftly amplify into a full-fledged rock 'n' roll riot, as bricks and bottles flew through the air, and car and store windows shattered.

The Morrison police department was hopelessly outnumbered; reinforcements were called in from as far afield as Jefferson County and even Denver. Morrison itself was closed off to prevent the crowd getting any larger, any stronger. And all the while the army within responded to police demands to disperse, with the chant "Hell no, we won't go."

And they wouldn't be invited back, either. Although there was no trouble at Red Rocks itself, the promoter, Barry Fey, was adamant that Phish would not be returning to the scene of so many past triumphs. His decision was applauded throughout the tiny community. Long since accustomed to these periodic influxes of rock 'n' roll fans, long since geared up for the night things might get out of hand, still Morrison was mortified when their fears were finally realized. Phish were old friends, Phish Heads were old friends. Of all the people in the world to abuse the town's hospitality, it had been the ones they trusted the most.

"We were waiting for an incident to happen," Morrison mayor Mary Poe told the *Rocky Mountain News*. "But we were hoping that nothing would." At the end of the day, though, "There were just way too many of them,"

Phish Head Doug Rotondo, looking back from six

months after the event, recalls, "Three thousand people con-
verged upon a city that isn't even the size of a city block, and
way more than half of them didn't have tickets to do anything
but schwill taddies and dance to 'Shakedown Street' bein'
bumped outta that phat microbus with the system in the back.
So, overpopulation was a bad thing.

"But you can't blame a girl getting hit on that. Because
my feeling is, had the man who was driving the truck *not*
tried to prove something to a group of 'very threatening'
young adults, then there would have been no incidents at
all. Don't forget, nothing went wrong the first day, or two
days after. And I say he was trying to prove something, because he was driving very fast in the obviously pedestrian-
laden streets. I would like to have seen what he was thinking
at the time.

"So, the police tried to clear the streets. I'm sure a lot of
you have heard that the whole situation boiled down to a
macho standoff, but what really was great was to see the fans
united to see if the sister was okay after she got hit. The whole
town stopped partying, and put our single needs aside for
someone who was in need of more. And then to see us stand
up for something that was ours. Something that was ours,
which someone else then tried to take away.

"It was hypocritical of the police to say, 'Okay, twenty
minutes ago you coulda been here . . . but now since this guy's
hit one of you, you don't have the right to be here anymore.'
And no matter how 'in control' the authorities think they had
it, lemme tell you, we allowed the situation to resolve. We
showed we were better than the police, and 'the law' for that
matter, because we didn't need to use force to get our point
across. We didn't need guns or horses, or SWAT teams—I
can't believe they brought them in to deal with us. But, we
were the bigger people is the bottom line. For those of you
reading this who were there that night, I thank you."

Many of the arrests were petty. One fan was apparently hauled off for informing the police, "You are slime." He was identified in the papers the next day as "twenty-one-year-old Marco Esquandolis," a character, of course, from "Run Like an Antelope," although the media didn't know that. Performing the song the following evening, and reaching the lyric in question, Trey could not resist throwing in a mischievous reference to a "twenty-one-year-old Phish fan."

In fact the newspapers seemed to be supplying Trey with a lot of inspiration that week. David Bowie's "Life on Mars?" snuck back into the set on the last night, a wry comment on the news that a fragment of fossilized fern had been discovered in a piece of old meteorite. It's a god-awful small affair, indeed.

Trey continued to play down the Red Rocks incident when *Entertainment Weekly*'s Jeff Gordinier caught up with him a couple of months later. "Yes, a kid did get hit by a car, and I feel terrible about that. I always feel terrible if anyone gets hurt at one of our concerts. But when you get that many people together, somebody is going to get hurt."

Such lighthearted resignation could not, however, disguise a very troubled outlook. Two nights after the riot, Phish's Red Rocks residency hit the headlines again as police caught on to a shipment of counterfeit tickets for that evening's show, flown into Denver International from, of all places, Mexico City. The moment Customs opened the package, they knew something was amiss. The moment Ticketmaster officials received a fax of one of the tickets, the game was up.

Phish moved on, to the Alpine Valley Music Theater in East Troy, Wisconsin. Trouble moved with them. In scenes horrifically reminiscent of the parking-lot massacres at Dead shows in the past, local lawmen simply donned tie-dye T-shirts, scruffy jeans, and swooped down on the venue. The fans' stupidity did the rest. A total of 195 arrests were made that day, most of them for possession or sale of marijuana, LSD, and psychedelic mushrooms. Four days later, another one hundred were picked up at Hershey Park Stadium. Patterns which grew all too familiar during the early 1990s seemed destined to continue into the second half of the decade.

Against this backdrop of growing tension and mounting paranoia, Phish closed their summer tour with the biggest show they had ever played—the Clifford Ball. Indeed, it was the country's largest concert event of the year, a two-day festival at Plattsburgh Air Force Base in Plattsburgh, New York. Over 135,000 tickets, at $20 and $30, were sold for the two-day festival, which peaked with three sets a day from Phish, amid a sprawling abecedarium of arts and amusements. A makeshift radio station kept the waiting crowds entertained; a prefab Clifford Chapel allowed one couple to get married. In the wee small hours of the second morning, Phish drove through the crowd on a flatbed truck and played a near-silent set to a crowd of insomniacs. Camera crews recorded everything.

Phish Head Tony DiMaggio remembers, "Where the fuck is Plattsburgh, New York? That was the main concern on a warm summer afternoon, as we began to pack up the car for a trip that will remain crisp in my mind better than any vacation I've ever been on. The weather couldn't have been better, the mood . . . excitement, joy, and a little nervousness. After all, it was my first Phish show, and Tom was the only other one out of us all who had seen a Phish show."

For Tony, Plattsburgh was a good six hours up I-87 from his New Jersey home. "So we spent most of the afternoon at Shop-Rite, Campmor, and Ramsey Outdoor. We had sleeping bags, coolers of beer, soda, food, and more beer, tents, stoves, lanterns, bug torches, and clothes. At around midnight Friday, we hit the road and embarked on what would be a sacred trip."

Stopping only to relieve themselves and refuel, they drove through the night, passing all the VW Westphalias with their Steal Your Face and dancing-bear stickers; bedded down at the campsite; then awoke after noon to discover 100,000 other people had arrived while they were sleeping.

"It was really strange," Tony continues. "Once I stepped out of the tent, I think I left something behind. I didn't have a care in the world. I forgot about my job, my house, my life back home. *I was at a Phish show*, that's all that mattered. In an ordinary situation, the crickets would have bothered me. I liked them. The real freaky people that lived off acid, trying to get that one miracle, would have bothered me, but not that weekend. Free hug . . . sure. Have a seat and chill awhile. The feeling is like nothing else in the world. Youth, energy, love, and fun.

"Six P.M.—Phish are coming on soon. We exchanged our tickets for wristbands and headed in. Mr. Sanity stepped out and welcomed us to the largest Phish show in the world. The cheers rang, and the chills ran through me—I'm going to have the time of my life. Phish busted out with 'Chalk Dust Torture.' Before I knew it I caught the groove, dancing around, jumping, singing, till I was at the point that I didn't know where any of my friends went. It was too early to worry about that.

"The next day was better than the first. Phish tore out tunes that I thought I would never hear: 'Wilson,' 'A Day in the Life,' 'Suzie Greenberg,' 'Tweezer,' 'Strange Design'. . . . After the show, we regrouped again. At around two A.M. some poor guy face-planted on a Hibachi that someone just barbecued off of, and he required some medical attention. We did what we could, but it was pretty bad and we sent him to First Aid. That was an amazing thing in itself. The layout was perfect. If you needed it, you could find it. Water, food, help, all the stupid things that you forget to bring. All with a stage for a backdrop, and a skyline so beautiful, I still haven't seen anything like it."

"The vibe . . . was just incredible," Trey raved. "The one thing we kept hearing over and over again was that no one had ever seen anything like this. We realized that there is another whole level of concerts that hasn't been explored yet."

The 1980s, he condemned, were all about money. "As a result, there were a lot of bands in the recording studio that didn't deserve to be there, and the general level of pop music went down. It has taken the industry ten years to heal itself, and now it seems like everyone is breathing better, and concerts are becoming more interesting again." And even though, he continued, "the media ignored it, . . . just like we weren't even there," shows like the Clifford Ball ensure that they will remain interesting.

The dilemmas facing Phish as they headed out to Woodstock to begin work on their seventh album were manifold. *A Live One* had, for many people, proved the consummate Phish album, the first record in their canon to capture the magic which they so freely distributed every night onstage; it was also, from Phish's point of view, the end of an era. They'd tried, just two years before, to create an album first and then allow the live show to develop out of it, and *Hoist* became their biggest-selling studio album as a consequence. The same modus operandi was in place for *Billy Breathes*, but with even less emphasis on how the songs would sound in concert. It was a rebirth, a reinvention.

Billy Breathes was originally conceived as Phish's first self-produced album. In February 1996, says Trey, "we checked into the Barn, at Bearsville Studios, with no preconceived notions. Just that it would be the four of us getting together.

The feeling was that we would stop trying so hard to capture the live show, and just let things come naturally."

Phish were originally planning to finally record the oft-promised and much anticipated Gamehendge CD-ROM. "It was all planned, wheels were in motion," reflects Trey. "But then we had this meeting and I said, 'I just don't want to think about anything old.'"

It was not only exhaustion which scuppered the project and sent the group searching for a new direction. Trey told *Billboard*, "It was like we had this giant eighteen-wheeler we started driving in first gear in the mid-1980s, and it kept picking up speed through the years, until last year it ended up hurtling down a mountainside with no driver. We needed to park the truck and start walking again."

The album sessions were disorganized. Trey and Tom Marshall were recently returned from a scuba vacation in the Cayman Islands, where they spent their non-aquatic hours writing songs; they returned home with a vast stockpile of twenty-seven. Few were finished masterpieces, however, which was where Phish's own sense of adventure came into play. Attempting to create songs in the most organic way possible, Mike describes, the band would start with one note— "We called it the Blob. We went around in a circle with one band member at a time adding a note. We didn't have to play our own instruments, and normal song structure didn't matter."

It was an audacious attempt to break down the regular conventions of songwriting, and, Page insists, "Songs started to develop on their own."

But where were they going? By mid-March, after almost a full month of laboriously piecing together workable music from such vague beginnings, Phish possessed a lot of workable ideas, a dozen basic tracks, but very little playable music. The Blob itself ran out of steam after about ten minutes.

"We hit a wall," Trey sighed. "We'd wanted to make an album that was just us, with nobody else hanging around. But then Page and I started working way too hard, doing all the stuff you have to do to make a record, but that, people don't know about. It got to the point where after you'd spent hours and hours comping tracks, you'd just want to leave. Then you'd record a track and it would sound completely exhausted." Page admits that it reached the stage where he was actually dreading returning to the studio every morning, because "All you could think of was, 'Oh God, I have to go back and listen to all this shit.' "

"Recording can be a tiring process," Trey understates, "so we took off for a month and looked at where we were. We decided we needed some outside perspective. . . ." And Elektra, who were watching developments with increasing unease, breathed a sigh of relief. "It was good to close the door awhile, so we could just play," Fish recalled; while Trey remarked later, "We fulfilled this need to be completely alone, recording again and hanging out. We needed to get our feet back on the ground." But they also learned why Phish needed a producer.

Three days before they were due to return to the studio, Phish contacted Steve Lillywhite, the legendary producer whose client list only began with U2, whose epochal first three albums he supervised. Since that time, he has worked with most of the giants of both modern and classic rock, from the Rolling Stones to Morrissey, from Talking Heads to the Dave Matthews Band. It was, in fact, Matthews himself who recommended Lillywhite to Phish, and with engineers Jon Siket and Chris Laidlaw already in place at the Barn, precisely the same team was regrouped, in precisely the same place, as had created the Matthews Band's *Crash*. The only question now was whether Lillywhite's rock sensibilities could even begin to meld with Phish's arcane convolutions.

That question was answered almost immediately. "Steve was perfect," Fish raved. "He brought a fresh energy that was very uplifting." He also brought what Trey calls "a new point of view, seeing and hearing things we normally wouldn't."

Mike told *Bass Player* magazine, "When we were producing ourselves, we were recording only three takes of a song at a time, because we found if we did five or six, the first or second would usually be the best. Steve, though, had us do about forty takes of each song!"

Fish continued, "I think we considered a lot of the things that made up our favorite albums, just good, tight, concise song arrangements, good strong melodies, good lyrics, we wanted all our lyrics to be good. We wanted the arrangements to be tight and to not meander. And we didn't want the songs to have a lot of fat. We wanted things to have different textures, just all these things that we've thought about and experienced about what makes an album good over the years of our existence. We wanted this album to have all these elements. We just sort of went in there with this sort of pure ideal of what a good album is." Lillywhite's expertise was invaluable in that respect, but equally important, the producer shared Phish's sense of the unexpected, and proved a more than willing ally as they threw commercial caution to the wind, time and time again.

When Nancy Jeffries, senior VP of A&R at Elektra, heard that Phish were going to close the album with "Strange Design," she was delighted. The song had been kicking around Phish's live set since May 1995, growing in the process into a veritable smash hit–in–waiting. Even more exciting, the band would record two versions of the song, one which adhered to the live version, which Mike insists was shaping up to be the best thing on the album; and a second, Beatles-esque take which everyone admitted was at least as catchy as hell.

So far as Jeffries was concerned, Phish had a major hit single already.

And then Phish threw it away. "Strange Design" was scrapped, and before Jeffries, or anyone else, could protest, Mike let them know it was the best thing they could have done. Phish knew the song was commercial, they knew it was a hit. But they also knew that if they took that route, they might never be able to backtrack again. Phish had made it this far on their own terms; they were not going to surrender now.

"Our original plan was to say 'fuck' every once in a while, so they wouldn't be able to play it on the radio," Mike revealed. But that would have been too cruel. Far better simply to dump "Strange Design" altogether.

With only a hint of despair in her voice, Jeffries admitted that after an experience like that, the label was simply going to leave Phish to their own devices. "I'm sure there were stages at Elektra in the past, where we looked at these growing audiences and said, 'Why aren't we selling more? Let's try to get out there and bust this.' But Phish kind of dictated the pace. So many people have tried and failed to change their course that we're better off to let it happen."

And it was happening very well. Without once reining in Phish's natural inclinations, Lillywhite brought his own vast experience to bear, pointing the music in directions that neither Phish nor past producers even dreamed of. "This album shows the benefit of us being a band for thirteen years," Fish explained. "We really got down to the essence of each song."

That essence swiftly found its level, too. *Billy Breathes*, raved *Rolling Stone* following the disc's November 1996 release, was "a quiet gem of an album . . . as rustic as the New England countryside, a warm declaration of optimism packaged in concise, radio-attractive songs." And that was despite the strange demise of "Strange Design"!

Entertainment Weekly was equally effusive. "*Billy Breathes* is a sweet, catchy, stripped-down song cycle in the spirit of Neil Young's *Harvest* and the Dead's *American Beauty.*" *Rolling Stone*'s chosen comparisons were *Workingman's Dead* and the Beatles' *Abbey Road*; other critics chose other reference points. But all ultimately went along with *Entertainment Weekly*. At the end of the day, Phish were "ripe for commercial breakthrough." Within days of release, *Billy Breathes* crashed onto the *Billboard* chart at number 7.

At last, the fortune tellers were proven correct; for three years now, industry insiders had sworn Phish were on the verge of a major chart smash, and as the predictions piled up prior to the album's release, Fish was groaning, "Oh no, not again."

He told the Pennsylvania-based *Gallery of Sound Gazette*, "I think the reason they seem to be saying this more about this album than any other album is because every year that goes by, more people know we exist. And this is due mostly to our live show. . . . The media has started to recognize that we exist, because we had this huge concert [the Clifford Ball] in the Northeast this summer that no one covered when it was happening. Everybody afterwards went, 'Wow, where did all these people come from? What is going on with this band?' So all of a sudden now, we're getting all the more attention.

"But [even] when *Hoist* came out, the president of Elektra was storming through the offices going, 'This is the album that's going to break them! This is the album that's going to be the hit!' And all these people, all the people that knew about us then, and any of the media who knew about us then, and anyone who was paying attention to us then, was saying exactly the same thing. There were just less people saying it."

Now, it seemed, everyone was saying it, and everyone was right.

Phish's fall tour kicked off as the first single from the

album, the effervescent "Free," hit the radio. Returning to the scenes of so many past triumphs, the band played a Halloween bash at the Atlanta Omni, which sold out in a record-breaking twelve minutes, two nights at the Philadelphia Spectrum, and finally, the year-end shows at Boston's Fleet Center.

Of course, it was Atlanta upon which the most attention was focused. In the weeks leading up to the show, the Internet buzzed with rumors, and every third person you met online was armed with their own inside track on which past classic would be revived by Phish: Zappa's *Joe's Garage* and Zeppelin's *Physical Graffiti* were the favorites, of course, but Pink Floyd's *Dark Side of the Moon* was also in with a shout, while there was more than one voice convinced, or at least hopeful, that it would be the same band's epic of indulgent chicanery, *Ummagumma*, with which Phish would regale the masses.

Whatever was planned, as the clock ticked down to show-time, Atlanta had never seen anything like it. Not even the Olympics were this crazy.

Harry Hood hustled past, flashing a grin at anyone who recognized him—and at everyone who didn't and thought he was just another custom-costumed freak. There were Fluffhead and Esther, a mass of glitter which could only be Sparkle, and someone who looked a dead ringer for U2's guitarist, with a Superman style *W* emblazoned on his chest—Is it a bird, is it a plane? No, it's Wedge. The whole city was like a costume ball, and it was impossible not to marvel at the power Phish possessed, the ease with which their music could transform the dullest clerk, the shrillest shop girl, into a creature of beauty and imagination.

Three boys dressed in greasy overalls passed, and a loud voice in the ticket queue sounded knowledgeably. "*Joe's Garage*," it confirmed. "It's the favorite by far." Someone else, equally loud, equally knowledgeable, laughed as the three passed through the crowd without a glance, continued on down the road, disappeared out of view. "Or maybe they just work there. And now they're going home."

Nevertheless, Zappa was the favorite. Everyone knew that, from the rugrats who sit on America On-Line all night, to the flight-deck commanders with the *Enterprise* in their bedrooms, and an immaculately filed cassette library of every Phish show that has ever been taped, and they could prove scientifically that this was Frank Zappa's year.

"It stands to reason." The loud voice from outside sounded even louder inside. "*Joe's Garage* was the people's choice last year, but Phish didn't think that they could do it justice then, so they held it over. No question about it." A few aisles away, a veritable posse of garage mechanics swept into view, a pair of grease monkeys, a pump boy, and a girl dressed as a car, with an INSERT NOZZLE HERE patch placed over her crotch. If it wasn't *Joe's Garage*, a lot of people had got their wires very crossed.

Once they came onstage, Phish knew the expectations they aroused, and they reveled in that knowledge. From the moment they first embarked upon this long, strange trip of their own, a Burlington quartet with no dreams wilder than making their music, Phish had sown the seeds of confusion, from the ROTC dance where they were chased offstage the moment they stopped playing, to the Boston nightclub they filled with their friends; from the first puzzled press mentions of a phenomenon in Vermont, to the best-kept secret in rock.

In 1996, Phish staged the largest concert to take place anywhere on the North American continent. In 1995, they were among the top twenty grossing attractions of the year. In 1994, they sold out Madison Square Garden in less time than it takes to buy a drink there. And still, one could go for weeks at a time without meeting anyone who's even heard of the band; who thinks Phish was the singer with Marillion; that Clifford Ball is a weird Olympic sport; and that Halloween is simply a case of Trick or Treat.

Well, they'd be right on that score, and as the first set spiraled toward its climax, Phish were adamant that their audience would be getting a taste of both.

Remain in Light was Talking Heads' fourth, and most successful, album. Released in October 1980, on the back of the insanely contagious "Once in a Lifetime" hit single, *Remain in Light* was also the third and final installment of the triptych of albums which the New Yorkers recorded with maverick ambient music producer Brian Eno, as jarring as anything the group (or producer) attempted in the past, but awash with the sensibilities which, in later years, Eno would bring to his work with U2.

Remain in Light was Mike Gordon's contribution to the catalog of albums Phish offered the fan club, and few of the people voting for the old faithful standbys, *Joe's Garage* included, gave it any chance of winning. Mike, though, felt that this might just be its year, and with it, the opportunity for Phish themselves to be catapulted beyond the era of classic rock with which they were most commonly associated.

Redolent of all those months Mike spent, so many years before, pounding the high-school boards with his New Wave hopefuls the Edge, but possessing more contemporary references too (through Talking Heads' associations with producer Steve Lillywhite who handled 1988's *Naked*), *Remain in Light* was also a reminder that though Phish's most commonly remarked-upon precedents were the heroes of the sixties and seventies jam generation, their roots were locked firmly in the modern age, and could scarcely have been anywhere else. Their influences are all over the show, but their line of descent is unimpeachably pure: Alice Cooper and Kiss, Elvis Costello and the Knack, Peter Gabriel and the Smiths. And of course, Talking Heads.

"Born Under Punches" opened Phish's second set in Atlanta, just as it opens the original album. Even as the crowd reeled from the shock, even as the hundred voices primed to greet the expected "Central Scrutinizer" faltered in mid-roar, "Born Under Punches" scratched open old memories, unearthed old emotions. There was no escape from this song in its prime; with a hallful of tape recorders silently whirling, there would be no escape from it in its dotage, either.

"Once in a Lifetime," the quirky slice of disco rock which singlehandedly cemented Talking Heads' reputation among rock's most adventurously art-stricken acts, sent things soaring up another notch, again in the same way it once highlighted Talking Heads sets. According to Chris Frantz, Talking Heads' drummer, "We used to have so much fun playing this song live. It was a soaring feeling and the audience was right there with us." So it was in Atlanta.

Later in the set, "Cross-Eyed and Painless" gave band and audience another opportunity to stretch out of their traditional confines. Talking Heads' own version of the song was heavily influenced by Kurtis Blow's seminal "These Are the Breaks" (Chris Frantz played on that as well), and Phish's performance reached right back to that urban archetype, even as it strived to ally the Talking Heads' grating idiosyncracies with their own musical brief. Far more than either the *White Album* or *Quadrophenia, Remain in Light* offered Phish the chance to prove their interpretative powers, and they grasped it with both hands.

But that, too, was something in which Phish were well versed now. For thirteen years, they had been out there taking chances, in every sense of the phrase. A last-minute opening on a small-town concert bill, a call to go out with other groups of their ilk, an invitation to join the most prestigious jazz festival in the country—Phish pride themselves in making music which knows no definable boundaries. It only follows that the places they take that music should be equally unrestricted. So long as there's an audience, and somewhere to plug in, Phish have never balked, and in that resolution, another sense has grown that more than any other American act which has labored beneath such an epithet, Phish are truly a people's band.

In an age when MTV rules the music scene, Phish refuse to even discuss making videos. At a time when success is measured by how many magazine covers you star on, Phish are rarely mentioned in the mainstream music press. And in an era when every entertainer must be neatly targeted at a so-specific audience, Phish have risen so far above the categories that even their fans cannot pin them down. They are an anomaly, but they are also a phenomenon.

And all this has been achieved without recourse to any of the conventional staples of rock promotion. To the public-at-large, Phish are absolute unknowns. But to a very large public, they are the ultimate counterculture mavericks, a brick through the jeweler's shop window, the greatest smash-and-grab act in the world.

It rather looks as though the game is up now, and all the world is out catching Phish. Forget Metallica and the Fugees, forget Oasis and Bon Jovi. "Forget Pearl Jam," *Entertainment Weekly* implored. "Phish, four jam-happy guys from Vermont, are the biggest band in America—no bones about it."

EPILOGUE: THIS LAST NIGHT IN SODOM

The street teemed with life, both low and getting higher. Shell McLennan lost count of the number of times she was asked for spare change as they crossed from the T, forgot that no matter how horrific the homeless were other times, the holiday season made them all look like birthday boys, and what was worse was that she couldn't summon up even an ounce of compassion for the legless vets or the toothless whores, or any one of the thousands of others she knew were sleeping in doorways and subway gates and heating vents, not because she didn't have pity for them, but because it wasn't her pity they wanted.

The outstretched hands that "brushed" her body, the stale-spirits breath and the breathless stale spirits, the fact that these people seemed to glory in their effrontery, all these things made her mind recoil as fast as her body, and she slipped an arm into Carl's, not for protection, but for reassurance, for the knowledge that not everybody in Beantown was out to shake you down for a quarter.

The Fleet Center loomed before her, and before it, the

assembled multitudes of Phish, in all their colors and costumes and clouds of make-believe, the new beautiful people with flowers in their hair, but with the benefit of having lived two decades after the tribes which preceded them. In 1967, the future was their parents' for the taking, but they had dropped the ball and kept running regardless, to be drawn up short when the new decade dawned, and the Who were blaring out of FM stations everywhere, *"Won't get fooled again!"*

For they were fooled, and they weren't going to get back to the garden, because it wasn't even a parking lot anymore. But they were all too blind and arrogant to see that, to understand that Jimi and Janis and Jerry and Jim and all those cats were wrong all along, because although they'd got the answers down pat, they hadn't quite grasped what the questions were yet.

Three decades on, the same faiths were back, the same beliefs, the same sense of love and we're all in this together right now, so we might as well start painting the walls.

The difference was, we'd lived a little longer, and dreamed and schemed and maybe we wouldn't be fooled again, but that's only because there's precious little left to put that much faith into. Nothing had changed, which meant that in all probability, nothing ever will. "I am not a cynic," Shell wrote in her diary one time. "I'm a realist. The world is fucked, but I'm willing to admit that." But as she embraced the familiar faces that passed her, and smiled at the ones who she thought would smile back, she knew she wasn't the only one.

A freak snagged her arm as she dug in one pocket for her billfold. He looked a little like the Dude of Life, or maybe that was the idea, but he asked her name and she laughed as she told him.

"Hey, Shell—and you've been to see Phish! Can I call you Shellphish?"

Oh, what the hell, it was New Year's Eve. She turned and smiled.

"You know, no one's ever thought of that before."

A SELECTION OF PHISH WEB SITES

Phish's online presence is one of the highest in the music industry; one search engine reported over 1,000 relevant sites. The following is a tiny sampling of the most interesting and varied at the time of this writing; new sites, however, are appearing constantly, and changes of address are not uncommon.

http://www.phish.com
The band's official page includes up-to-the-minute news, tour info, and merchandising details.

http://www.phish.net
"For Phish fans, by Phish fans," the Phish Net includes song lyrics, tape details, and, of course, the *Helping Friendly Book*.

http://www.oe.org
Operation Everyshow is the home page for a ruthlessly regimented tapers organization.

http://www.elektra.com
Elektra Records's Phish page offers a discography, sound clips, and more.

http://www.cec.wustl.edu/-hewins/phish/phish.html
News and plenty of links to other Phish sites.

http://www.ihoz.com/phishstats.html
ZZYZX's Phish Stats is an interactive program allowing one to build statistical reports of Phish performances, by song, locale, and so on.

http://www.chessworks.com/phish.html
A fascinating analysis of Phish's chess games.

http://www.nerdworld.com/users/dstein/nw221.html
Phish by Nerd World Media offers one of the largest collections of links.

http://www.phish.org
WWW.Phish.Org presents some great graphics, a handy "Answers" section, and the complete Gamehendge saga.

PHISH DISCOGRAPHY

1985: Untitled Studio Session (unreleased)
And So to Bed / You Enjoy Myself / Green Dolphin Street /
Harry Hood / Slave to the Traffic Light / Run Like an An-
telope / Divided Sky / Letter to Jimmy Page / Fluffhead (live)

1987: The White Album (unreleased)
Alumni Blues > Steve Reich / And So to Bed / You Enjoy
Myself / AC/DC Bag / Fuck Your Face / Divided Sky / Slave
to the Traffic Light / Aftermath / Ingest / N20 / Fluff's Trav-
els / Dog Log / Hamburger / Run Like an Antelope / Minkin
/ Letter to Jimmy Page

1988: The Man Who Stepped into Yesterday (unreleased)
Wilson Chant > narration > Lizards > Tela > narration >
Wilson > narration > AC/DC Bag > narration > Colonel
Forbin's Ascent > Famous Mockingbird > narration > The
Sloth > narration > Possum

1989: Junta (original release)
Fee / You Enjoy Myself / Esther / Golgi Apparatus / Foam

/ Dinner and a Movie / Divided Sky / David Bowie / Fluff-head (Fluff's Travels / The Chase / Who Do We Are / Clod / Bundle of Joy / Arrival) / Contact

1990: Lawn Boy (original release: Absolute A-Go-Go Records)

The Squirming Coil / Reba / My Sweet One / Split Open and Melt / Oh Kee Pa Ceremony / Bathtub Gin / Run Like an Antelope / Lawn Boy / Bouncing Around the Room / Fee

1992: Picture of Nectar (Elektra)

Llama / Eliza / Cavern / Poor Heart / Stash / Manteca/ Guelah Papyrus / Magilla / The Landlady / Glide / Tweezer / The Mango Song / Chalk Dust Torture / Faht / Catapult / Tweezer Reprise

1992: Junta (Elektra rerelease)

Fee / You Enjoy Myself / Esther / Golgi Apparatus / Foam / Dinner and a Movie / Divided Sky / David Bowie / Fluff-head (Fluff's Travels / The Chase / Who Do We Are / Clod / Bundle of Joy / Arrival) / Contact / Union Federal / Sanity (live) / Icculus (live)

1990: Lawn Boy (Elektra rerelease)

The Squirming Coil / Reba / My Sweet One / Split Open and Melt / Oh Kee Pa Ceremony / Bathtub Gin / Run Like an Antelope / Lawn Boy / Bouncing Around the Room

1993: Rift (Elektra)

Rift / Fast Enough for You / Lengthwise > Maze / Sparkle / Horn / The Wedge / My Friend My Friend / Weigh / All Things Reconsidered / Mound / It's Ice / Lengthwise / The Horse > Silent in the Morning

1994: Hoist (Elektra)

Julius / Down with Disease / If I Could / Riker's Mailbox / Axilla (Part II) / Lifeboy / Sample in a Jar / Wolfman's Brother / Scent of a Mule / Dog-Faced Boy / Demand

1995: *A Live One (Elektra)*

Bouncing Around the Room / Stash / Gumbo / Montana / You Enjoy Myself / Chalk Dust Torture / Slave to the Traffic Light / Wilson / Tweezer / Simple / The Squirming Coil

1996: Billy Breathes (Elektra)

Free / Character Zero / Waste / Taste / Cars, Trucks and Buses / Talk / Theme from the Bottom / Train Song / Bliss / Billy Breathes / Swept Away / Steep / Prince Caspian